15: PERSPECTIVES IN CRITICISM

PERSPECTIVES IN CRITICISM

15:

Ralph Wilson Rader

Tennyson's Maud: The Biographical Genesis

UNIVERSITY OF CALIFORNIA PRESS
Berkeley and Los Angeles
1963

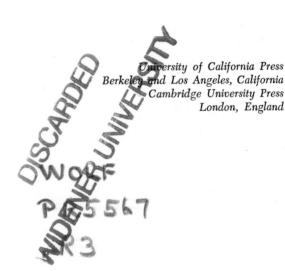

University of California Press
Berkeley and Los Angeles, California
Cambridge University Press
London, England

LIBRARY OF CONGRESS CATALOG CARD NUMBER: 63-20984
Printed in the United States of America
Designed by Ward Ritchie

To Robert Liddell Lowe

For now the Poet cannot die,
    Nor leave his music as of old,
    But round him ere he scarce be cold
Begins the scandal and the cry:

"Proclaim the faults he would not show;
    Break lock and seal, betray the trust;
    Keep nothing sacred, 'tis but just
The many-headed beast should know."

He gave the people of his best;
    His worst he kept, his best he gave.
    My Shakespeare's curse on clown and knave
Who will not let his ashes rest!

Who make it seem more sweet to be
    The little life of bank and brier,
    The bird that pipes his lone desire
And dies unheard within his tree,

Than he that warbles long and loud
    And drops at Glory's temple-gates,
    For whom the carrion vulture waits
To tear his heart before the crowd!

Preface

THIS BOOK was born out of the curiosity aroused in me by Tennyson's *Maud* and "Locksley Hall," ostensibly dramatic poems which were strangely flawed, I always felt, by some hidden emotional connection with the poet's own life. What was it? I began a systematic search for the answer under the stimulus of a seminar at Indiana University conducted by Professor Donald Smalley. Interest and comprehension grew simultaneously, then and later, as bits and pieces of evidence fitted together to justify tentative inferences. A trip to England and fuller investigation brought, not the conclusive documentation I had hoped for, but enough new facts to extend and validate the views I had been developing. The final result of my inquiry is this book. I hope that it gives the reader some sense of the excitement that went into its making, but I hope also that it brings, beyond that, understanding and sympathy for the great poet its subject, who would not have liked the book at all.

I wish to thank here the many people who helped me to produce this study, first of all Sir Charles Tennyson, who has given me, over the past four years, a great deal of encouragement, advice, and helpful criticism. More than that, as students of Tennyson will recognize, my book is everywhere indebted to his writings on his grandfather, without which indeed it would not have been begun. Donald Smalley gave my study its initial impetus and has given other aid since; James H. Sledd posed illuminating queries during the early stages of my investigation; James M. Cox revived my confidence when it was lagging. W. D. Paden offered some helpful facts and a welcome comment, quoted below. My colleagues John E. Jordan, Norman Rabkin, John H. Raleigh, and Wayne Shumaker have severally read my manuscript and given useful suggestions and advice. Mr. Christopher Ricks, of Worcester College, Oxford, has also read the manuscript and saved me from several errors. To all these men I am grateful. I am grateful also to Henry Nash Smith for help of a different kind, and to James A. Work, whose premature death in 1961 took from me a dear friend and kind benefactor.

Commander Sir John and Lady Maitland very graciously gave me an opportunity to inspect their beautiful Harrington Hall and its grounds, showed me many kindnesses, and answered many questions. Commander and Mrs. Hans Hamilton welcomed me to Somersby Rectory. Mrs. R. D. Shafto was equally kind in her hospitality and in allowing me to look over the papers, portrait, and library of her grandmother. Mrs. Susan Rawnsley gave me access to useful papers. Mrs. G. Fenwick-Owen supplied helpful reminiscences. Mr. R. F. N. Thoyts solicited from Mr. M. Reader the interesting letter which I quote in the text. Canon P. B. G. Binnall, Sir Francis Hill, and Charles Wilson offered long and pleasant conversation about Tennyson and Lincolnshire from which I learned much. To these three men and to the others named, I give my thanks.

Mrs. Joan Varley and her staff at the Lincolnshire Archives Office (particularly Mr. Michael Lloyd) were extremely helpful to me during my extended visit there and have shown even greater kindness since in patiently responding to a stream of letters requiring the checking of quotations and references; for their indispensable aid

viii

thanks are scarcely sufficient. I have received much help also from the staffs of the British Museum, the Houghton Library, Harvard, and Trinity College Library, Cambridge. I thank them especially, but also the Bodleian Library and the libraries of University College, London; Cambridge University; Duke University; Yale University; and the University of California, Berkeley.

I must not forget to thank too J. R. K. Kantor, my research assistant during the early stages of my investigation, who gave me a great deal of help, as did his successors Vern Bailey and Patrick Sullivan. And thanks of a very special kind go to my friends, Mr. and Mrs. Harry Leicht, for making my stay in England an especially pleasant one. Others who gave assistance in other ways include Sir Edward Malet, Bt., Hugh Richmond, Mrs. Elsie Duncan-Jones and Mrs. C. M. Duncan-Jones, and Edgar F. Shannon, Jr.

I am much indebted to the present Lord Tennyson for allowing me to quote from Hallam Lord Tennyson's *Memoir,* from the unpublished *Materials for a Life of A. T.,* and from the poet's unpublished letters and poems. Sir Charles Tennyson has also very kindly allowed me to quote without restriction from his *Alfred Tennyson* and the *Unpublished Early Poems.* Others to whom I am grateful for permission to quote from manuscript materials include Mrs. Dorothy Massingberd, Mrs. R. D. Shafto, Mrs. E. C. Tennyson d'Eyncourt, Duke University Library, Harvard College Library, and the library of Trinity College, Cambridge. My thanks go also to Macmillan and Co., Ltd., and St. Martin's Press, Inc., for permitting extensive quotation from Hallam Tennyson's *Tennyson and His Friends* and from the notes to his edition of his father's *Works,* and to The Macmillan Company and St. Martin's Press for quotations from Sir Charles Tennyson's *Alfred Tennyson.*

Section i of chapter 1 of this book originally appeared

as "The Composition of Tennyson's *Maud*" in *Modern Philology*, LIX (May, 1962), 265–269; section ii of the same chapter as "Tennyson in the Year of Hallam's Death," *PMLA*, LXXVII (September, 1962), 419–424; and chapter 2 as "Tennyson and Rosa Baring," *Victorian Studies*, V (March, 1962), 224–260. I should like to thank the editors of all three periodicals and, in the case of *Modern Philology*, the University of Chicago Press, for permission to reprint. I have taken the opportunity to remove, silently, various small errors in these original versions and have, of course, adjusted them in other minor ways to the requirements of my present text.

Finally, I should like to record my gratitude to the American Council of Learned Societies for a grant-in-aid which allowed me to make my trip to England, and to President Clark Kerr of the University of California for granting me a Faculty Summer Fellowship, without which I would have been unable to complete the writing of this book.

R. W. R.

Contents

1

Introductory

OF ALL his poems, *Maud* was peculiarly dear to Tennyson. Throughout his long later life, it was the poem he loved best to read aloud and the one he read most often and most powerfully; it was, above all, the one he most wished others to feel and understand. Shortly after the poem was published, for instance, a perplexed and annoyed Mrs. Carlyle watched Tennyson going about at Lady Ashburton's "asking everybody if they like his *Maud*—and reading *Maud* aloud" and endlessly "talking Maud, Maud, Maud." Earlier, at Chelsea, he had forced her to approve the poem by reading it to her three times in insistent succession; so that now, used though she was to his crotchets, she thought his actions odd indeed. He was "strangely excited about *Maud*," she said—"as sensitive to criticisms as if they were imputations on his honor." [1] Time brought no change in Tennyson's attitude, for a month before his death he exhausted himself in a special reading arranged for the edification of critic Henry Van Dyke, who had written unfavorably of the poem; Van Dyke went away overwhelmed and awed by the passion of the old poet's performance. [2] But all Tennyson's recitations showed the intensity of his involvement in the poem. Rossetti describes a reading in which the poet shed tears and felt obviously strong emotion, and we hear of another occasion on which he read the poem

1

"with such intensity of feeling that he seized and kept quite unconsciously twisting in his powerful hands a large brocaded cushion which was lying at his side." [3] "There was a peculiar freshness and passion in his reading of 'Maud,'" his son writes, "giving the impression that he had just written the poem, and that the emotion which created it was fresh in him. This had an extraordinary influence on the listener, who felt that the reader had been *present* at the scenes he described, and that he still felt their bliss or agony." [4]

How is Tennyson's deep engagement in his poem to be explained? Few critics have thought the poem completely successful as a work of art; recognizing the beauty of the lyrical passages, most of them have found the love story of the poem strained and unreal, while the emotion in the work has struck them, despite Tennyson's protestations, as uncomfortably raw and dramatically uncontrolled. Did this strange poem hold some deeply private meaning for Tennyson that he loved it so intensely? My attempt in this study will be to show that it did and that we can in some measure understand what the meaning was. But before we can deal with the poem as an autobiographical expression, we must go a circuitous journey from the composition of the poem, back twenty years in Tennyson's life and forward again, through some obscure episodes in it, once more to the time of writing. In the process we shall learn some new and interesting facts about Tennyson, but our final subject, in the last chapter, will be *Maud* itself.

I

The relationship of *Maud* to Tennyson's own experience has been obscured by the apparent circumstances of its composition, for, according to a well-known story, repeated by all the biographers, the poem was written almost by chance at the suggestion and urging of a

2

friend. Aubrey de Vere gives the most detailed account in Hallam Tennyson's *Memoir:*

> In 1854 I went from Swainston, the residence of Sir John Simeon, . . . to Farringford, where the poet then made abode with his wife and two children. The eldest was about two years old; the other an infant in arms; . . . Tennyson was engaged on his new poem "Maud." Its origin and composition were, as he described them, singular. He had accidentally lighted upon a poem of his own which begins, "O that 'twere possible," and which had long before been published in a selected volume got up by Lord Northampton for the aid of a sick clergyman. It had struck him, in consequence, I think, of a suggestion made by Sir John Simeon, that, to render the poem fully intelligible, a preceding one was necessary. He wrote it; the second poem too required a predecessor; and thus the whole work was written, as it were, *backwards*.[5]

Tennyson himself substantiates this account in a note on the poem: "'O that 'twere possible' appeared first in the *Tribute,* 1837. Sir John Simeon years after begged me to weave a story round this poem, and so *Maud* came into being."[6] Simeon's part in the process is elaborated by his daughter, Mrs. Louisa Ward:

> The writing and publication of "Maud" in 1855 was largely due to my father.
>
> Looking through some papers one day at Farringford with his friend, he came upon the exquisite lyric "O that 'twere possible," and said, "Why do you keep these beautiful lines unpublished?" Tennyson told him that the poem had appeared years before in the *Tribute,* an ephemeral publication, but that it was really intended to belong to a dramatic poem which he had never been able to carry out. My father gave him no

3

peace till he had persuaded him to set about the poem, and not very long after, he put "Maud" into his hand.[7]

These statements, the source of almost all subsequent accounts, have always been treated as if they agreed completely with one another, but obviously they do not. Mrs. Ward attributes the rediscovery of "O that 'twere possible" to Simeon but says that the plan of an extended poem was already in Tennyson's mind, while de Vere says that the poet "accidentally" made the discovery himself but that Simeon suggested the extension at some indefinite later time. Tennyson's offhand note is too cryptic to clear up the discrepancies, but the differences in the de Vere and Ward accounts, though seemingly trivial, in fact indicate that the story they have jointly been presumed to tell is a considerable oversimplification of what must actually have happened.[8]

In the first place there is a less well-known version of the origin of *Maud* given by W. F. Rawnsley:

It was at Shiplake [in 1852 or 1853?] . . . that on his casting about, as he often did, for a new subject to write on, my mother, as she herself told me, suggested his enlarging his lovely little fragment, published some years before in "The Tribute," than which she told him he had never written anything better, and which, for he acted on the suggestion, is now imbedded in "Maud." . . . I have seen the whole canto as it then stood, written out at the time for my mother.[9]

How is this statement to be reconciled with the Simeon story? Mrs. Rawnsley may indeed have spoken without effect and wrongly assumed, when *Maud* came out two or three years later, that its writing was owing to her when in fact it was owing to Simeon. But it seems quite unlikely even then that the two friends would separately and at random have hit upon this obscure early poem and suggested an extension without any help from Tennyson. If, however, the idea of an extension

4

had been for some time in Tennyson's own mind (as Mrs. Ward's account implies), his talk of his plans might have given both friends the basis for their suggestions. This plausible supposition is supported by the earliest written record of the poem's origin, an account given by Rossetti in August, 1855, in a letter to William Allingham: "I dare say that you know that *Maud* originated in the section, 'Would that 'twere possible,' etc., which was printed in an annual years ago and was liked so much (as one hears) by T.'s friends that he kept it in view and gradually worked it up into the story." [10] If Rossetti's remark is an accurate gloss on the apparent contradictions of the other accounts, it explains certain facts in the history of *Maud* which are otherwise difficult to account for.

The germinal "O that 'twere possible" was written, not in 1837, but soon after the death of Arthur Hallam in late 1833. [11] The original version, extant in several manuscripts, is nearly the same as the version which later appeared in *Maud* but is considerably shorter than the 1837 version printed in the *Tribune*. The reasons for the 1837 extension are clear from the circumstances of the publication. Richard Monckton Milnes had solicited a contribution to the *Tribune* from Tennyson (for the purpose noted by de Vere) but had got in reply what he considered, somewhat unreasonably, an insulting refusal. Milnes' angry response so shocked and surprised the poet that he sent back a conciliatory letter which ended with a promise to send a contribution after all. He was slow in fulfilling his promise, however, and Milnes wrote once more to stir him up. Tennyson replied: "I have *not* been forgetful; these two poems have been causing me infinite bother to get them into shape; one I cannot send: it is too raw, but as I have made the other double its former size, I hope it will do. I vow to Heaven I never will have to do with these books again—so never ask me." [12] The "other" poem was, of course, "O that 'twere possible." Clearly, then, Tennyson finished and published his poem in 1837 against his will, cobbling up an ending for it under pressure because he wished to pacify Milnes and had no other poem to do it with. But that he continued to think of his poem as incomplete (the 1834 version ended unsatisfactorily with "And weep / My whole soul out to thee") is suggested by the existence of a fair copy, dated April, 1838, in which it has been returned to its pre-1837 form; [13] and by the fact that he did not reprint this lovely lyric in the 1842 volumes or in any other collection before *Maud*. The *Tribute* publication, consequently, did not mean for Tennyson that he was done with "O that 'twere possible," and we need not imagine that he forgot it till Mrs. Rawnsley or Simeon brought it to his notice. In the years after 1837 Tennyson probably did keep the poem "in view" and may from time to time have talked to friends about his intention to work it up into a long "dramatic poem," which he nevertheless was not "able to carry out"; and so it might have been that Mrs. Rawnsley had the opportunity to make her suggestion.

But whatever Tennyson's specific intentions in those years, it is clear that before his intimacy with Simeon began (and probably not long after his conversation with Mrs. Rawnsley), he had turned his mind back to the poem that eventually grew into *Maud*. Simeon first called on the Tennysons, the *Memoir* tells us, "on the day of Lionel's christening." [14] Now Lionel was born March 16, 1854, and it has always been assumed that the christening—and the meeting with Simeon—came shortly after; actually, Lionel was not christened, because of his mother's ill health, till June 6,[15] so that Simeon's suggestion must have been made sometime after that date. But on October 12, 1853, Henry Sellwood had written in a letter to his daughter Emily: "Not knowing any one who would work cheaper than myself I have copied & now send you Alfred's poem from the tribute." [16] Attached is a manuscript of the poem and below the body of the letter is a penciled notation in an unidentified hand, "Maud is based upon this poem sent." The notation must have been made by someone close to Tennyson, but even without it one can see that the poem was not "accidentally lighted upon," as de Vere has it, but purposely sent for; and, more important, that Tennyson plainly intended to do something with the piece eight months before his friendship with Simeon began.

But Tennyson not only intended but actually did begin to compose the poem before he knew Simeon. In the notes to *Maud* he records that Part III was "written when the cannon was heard booming from the battleships in the Solent before the Crimean War," [17] which began on March 24, 1854. Since, as we now know, Simeon did not visit the Tennysons till June 6, the discrepancy between this note and the usual story is obvious. But there is some uncertainty about the note; a letter Tennyson wrote late in April to Coventry Patmore seems to contradict it. Patmore had apparently written to suggest that Tennyson was the author of some newspaper verses about the Baltic fleet, which had assembled just before the war off the Isle of Wight. Tennyson replied: "The Baltic fleet I never saw! not a vessel: not a line have I written about it or the war. Some better things I have done, I think successfully." [18] Patmore's editor comments that this statement is "of interest as showing that none of the war passages in 'Maud,' had been written at this time." This is too broad an inference. Tennyson did not think of Part III as "about" the war in the journalistic sense that Patmore intended; [19] and the "better things" he speaks of could have been parts of *Maud*. Other evidence, moreover, supports Tennyson's statement in the notes. Cannonadings such as the one which fixed itself in his memory were common in the Solent before the war. One such is recorded in Emily's journal under February 8, and the same source tells us that on March 16, the day of Lionel's birth, Tennyson saw Mars culminating in the Lion, an event alluded to in Part III when the spirit-Maud points to "Mars / As he glow'd like a ruddy shield on the Lion's breast." [20] More than this, Part III seems clearly to echo contemporary newspaper accounts describing the very Baltic fleet which Tennyson denied to Patmore that he had written about. He seems, in fact, to have thought of his hero as taking specific part in the Spithead embarkation which followed the gathering of the fleet, for the "giant deck" on which the hero stands would be that of the *Duke of Wellington,* the great, newly commissioned man-of-war which the newspapers dwelt upon at length as "a giant ship" and "the largest ship in the world." Similarly, the "battle cry" of the "loyal people" in which the hero joins corresponds to the "thrilling and ungoverned burst of enthusiastic loyalty" ("a remarkable cheer— one which may be heard once, but never forgotten in a lifetime") which went up from the crews of the fleet as they were reviewed by Victoria on March 12.[21] Despite the letter to Patmore, Part III must have been written, as Tennyson's note says, three months before Simeon paid his first call at Farringford.

But Tennyson could hardly have written these verses, tailored as they are to the character and situation of his highly strung hero, without some idea of their place in a larger dramatic framework. And since Part III is unintelligible without reference to the story begun in "O that 'twere possible," it must from the first have been specifically intended as an extension of that poem. But whether Tennyson in the spring of 1854 proceeded any further with the hybrid work thus begun is not certain. At least two of the *Maud* lyrics—the "shell" verses and "Go not, happy day"—had been written earlier,[22] but probably with no thought of *Maud* in mind. And possibly Part I, iv, i, with its lines, "A million emeralds break from the ruby-budded lime / In the little grove where I sit," was written in April, 1854, since Tennyson at that time took particular notice of the blossoming limes in his Farringford garden.[23] But until an extensive collation of the widely scattered manuscripts of *Maud* is made, it would be difficult to move beyond conjecture in dating the other sections.

Probably, though, he did not get very far with the poem in the spring. The two sections he had before him —sharply contrasting in verse form, still fragmentary as narrative—would not have looked very promising, and, after occupying himself with the project in the winter and spring of 1853–1854, he must certainly have given it up. Otherwise, indeed, the Simeon story would make no sense. Sometime after Tennyson had laid the poem aside, then, Simeon must have seen the springtime worksheets of the poem (Mrs. Ward's "papers"?), including perhaps Henry Sellwood's copy of "Stanzas," and, learning that they were "intended to belong to a dramatic poem which [Tennyson] had never been able to carry out," he must have encouraged the poet to go on with the project by pointing out the need for the earlier story, which Tennyson must then have "written backwards" from the ending already completed.[24] But just when (after June 6) this intervention took place is not clear. According to F. T. Palgrave, *Maud* was "in course of completion" during September, 1854,[25] a statement implicitly supported by de Vere's account and by Emily's manuscript journal, which indicates that the poem was in at least tentative final form by November 1.[26] But, despite the fact that the poem had progressed so far by November, Simeon probably did not make his suggestion before Tennyson's return from his trip to Somersetshire in the first two weeks or so of August,[27] for the locale of the trip suggests that he was not yet involved again with the *Maud* poems but had turned his thoughts rather to his long-projected Arthurian epic. It seems unlikely that Tennyson would have interrupted with such a trip the compelling inspiration which Simeon's prompting, when it came, apparently aroused in him. Since after his return he "saw a great deal of the Simeons," [28] and since Mrs. Ward's account implies that the poem was composed very quickly (". . . not very long after, he put 'Maud' into his hand"), the most reasonable conclusion on the whole is that Simeon's suggestion came, as I have suggested, sometime in the latter part of August. To place it later rather than earlier in the acquaintance of the two men also allows for a greater lapse of time between Tennyson's work of the spring and his work of the fall, and thus makes it more plausible, the poem having been laid by for so long, that Simeon should later be remembered as its "onlie begetter."

Such, as best they can be made out after the lapse of more than a hundred years, are the facts of the origin of *Maud*. They are valuable not because they tell the slight truth that this or that friend was more or less responsible for Tennyson's writing the poem than has been thought, or that it was begun under different circumstances than has been supposed, but because they enable us to see that Tennyson's own involvement in the production of his poem was much more complex than his note or de Vere's account implies. In the accepted stories Tennyson seems nearly passive: the lost poem is rediscovered; Tennyson is badgered until he makes the extension almost against his will. Now we see that *Maud*, partially conceived, perhaps, as early as the fall of 1833, had been gestating in Tennyson's mind for a considerable period before Simeon's final act of midwifery brought it to birth. It was not produced by the accidental recovery of an ephemeral early lyric and the insistence of a friend but was very probably the long-purposed accomplishment of an inchoate, frustrated, but persistent intention. The revised account thus accords with what a sensitive reading of *Maud* tells us and with what we infer from Tennyson's own manifest feelings about the poem—that it was for him a very special kind of document with deep roots in his emotional being. The soil in which those roots were lodged was the experience of the twenty years since he had written the core lyric of the poem, a period initiated by the most decisive event of his life, the death of Arthur Hallam.

II

In the early 1830's, after his troubled youthful life, Tennyson had oriented himself intellectually and emotionally by fixing on the figure of Hallam. When Arthur died, not only did the inexplicable event shake his faith in the nature of things, but it also left him largely without the comfort, guidance, and support which his spirit demanded and which Hallam had been uniquely qualified to give. We do not, I believe, fully appreciate the nature and complexity of his attempt to recoup that loss. *In Memoriam,* first of all, has made it easy to imagine Tennyson's life in the years after 1833 as completely dominated by the fact of the death—as an uneventful and homogeneous expanse of slowly lightening sorrow extending indefinitely toward the 1840's and ending, temporarily at least, with the poet's engagement to Emily Sellwood. The loose, chronologically vague account in the *Memoir,*[29] together with a notable absence of documents from the period, has made such a notion easy to sustain. Sir Charles Tennyson's biography, however, has now sharpened and integrated our conception of this period and filled it out with new materials, so that an uncomplicated view of it is no longer possible. But even yet, because the documentary record is still so sparse, we assign perhaps too decisive an influence to Hallam's death and underemphasize other, secondary but very important developments which, following upon and reinforcing the effect of his loss, became intimately associated with it. Since an understanding of these developments will eventually be crucial to our understanding of *Maud,* it is fortunate that the 1833–1835 diary of Tennyson's friend, the Reverend John Rashdall, survives to fill out somewhat the factual record. Together with other contemporary papers it enables us to gauge more accurately than hitherto has been possible the nature and duration of Tennyson's immediate reaction to Hallam's death and so by inference to estimate more precisely the effect of those other events which came soon after.

Rashdall, who had been Tennyson's friend at Cambridge, was in 1833–1834 curate of Orby, a hamlet ten miles or so from Somersby Rectory; during his residence there he renewed his friendship with the poet and from time to time made brief notes of their meetings in his diary. An intelligent clergyman of pronounced Evangelical leanings, Rashdall was, in October, 1833, just settling down at Orby and beginning to make acquaintance in the neighborhood. On October 10 —ten days after the news of Hallam's death arrived at Somersby—he met Mary Tennyson, Alfred's eldest sister, at a dinner in a nearby home and from her heard the tragic news. His reaction, as recorded in the diary, is not altogether what one might expect: "Hallam is dead!—such is life: the accomplished–vain philosophic Hallam, dead, suddenly—at 23.—Indeed, true philosophy ought always to be saying—One thing is needful!" [30]

Two weeks later, after a visit from Alfred's eldest brother Frederick, Rashdall, more properly affected by the event, set down the earliest record we have of the Tennysons' reaction to their loss:

> His [Frederick's] Sister [Emily Tennyson, Hallam's fiancée] is of course in deepest misery as well as poor Hallam's Father, who says he has now nothing left but "to love those whom he loved," and that Emily as one to whom his Son was attached will always be to him an object of the most sacred regard. He will perhaps do something for her, or Alfred: Money for a Tour would be desir-

able to occupy her mind:—I can hardly conceive a greater calamity.[31]

Six days later the Tennysons' cousin Julia wrote to her brother George: "Poor Emily Tennyson is in great affliction by the sudden death of Mr. Hallam at Vienna of apoplexy & all the Somersby family seem to feel it severely." [32] Despite the fact that Alfred has always seemed by far the most prominent figure in that circle of mourners, one notices that neither here—nor elsewhere in the contemporary comments—is his grief singled out from that of the family generally; at the time Emily's response alone called special attention to itself.

Rashdall saw Frederick more than once in the weeks which followed, but he did not at first see Alfred. For a brief time the poet was probably in seclusion at Somersby, finding solace in the writing of verse. Very early in October his grief found its first poetic expression in the "Fair Ship" verses (later Section IX of *In Memoriam*) and, towards the end of the month, in the first draft of "Ulysses," [33] a work which he later said was "more written with the feeling of [Hallam's] loss upon me than many poems in 'In Memoriam.'" [34] About this time, too, he must have begun "The Two Voices," [35] so that all in all his poetic activity in these first days of grief is remarkable. More surprising, however, is the fact that within three weeks of Hallam's death he was in London, as a letter written October 25 by Edward FitzGerald shows. Whether he came to seek comfort among friends or to visit Arthur's family, FitzGerald does not say: "Tennyson has been in town for some time: he has been making fresh poems, which are finer, they say, than any he has done. But I believe he is chiefly meditating on the purging and subliming of what he has already done: and repents that he has published at all yet." [36] Why FitzGerald should speak thus of Tennyson without mentioning Hallam's death (of which he certainly knew through their mutual friend,

James Spedding) or Tennyson's sorrow, one does not know.

After visiting London Tennyson stopped at Cambridge to see Stephen Spring Rice, R. J. Tennant, and other friends.[37] His mood may be gauged from a letter Tennant sent him a few weeks later:

> I wish I were gifted with a far sight to reach over hills and towns even as far as Somersby and thro' the windows of the house, that I might see you, how you look when you come down to breakfast, and after breakfast whether you sit reading, writing or musing, whether you are gloomy or cheerful; I hope the latter; and that you can look back upon the mournful past without that bitterness of spirit which you felt when I saw you.[38]

On November 27, the day after Tennant wrote his letter, Rashdall attended a dinner at a Major Brackenbury's where a young lady (who happened to be Anthony Trollope's sister) [39] "argued with me ag[ains]t Alfred Tennyson with some vivacity." [40] We would not have expected to find Tennyson so engaged a little less than two months after the news of Hallam's death,[41] nor would we perhaps have expected him even to dine with Rashdall, as he did five days later. Yet these brief glimpses of him agree with the semi-jocular letters he was writing at the time [42] in suggesting that he had by late November and early December begun to gain control over his early grief. He could even think vaguely, as he wrote Kemble, "of coming up to Cambridge and attending your lectures next term." [43] More explicit evidence of Tennyson's recovery is a letter Frederick Tennyson wrote on December 28 to his cousin George. "As to myself," the elder brother says, "I am still at home pretty much in statu quo,—so is Alfred who will most probably publish again in the Spring." [44] Yet, as Frederick goes on to a most interesting assessment of the family's attachment to Hallam, he indicates that the implied adjustment was minimal:

14

You have probably heard before this from other sources the sad intelligence of the melancholy death of our dear friend Hallam, & the consequent affliction into which our family, especially Emily, has been plunged. We all looked forward to his society & support through life in sorrow & in joy, with the fondest hopes, for never was there a human being better calculated to sympathize with & make allowance for those peculiarities of temperament & those failings to which we are liable, —His loss therefore is a blow from which you may well suppose, we shall not easily recover.

From late December onward, Rashdall's diary shows, Tennyson and his family were increasingly active in a social way. One or two references, indeed, evoke images which sort rather oddly with the grimly monochromatic tableaux of the corresponding sections of *In Memoriam*. On December 26, for instance, the day after the somber "First Christmas" of the poem, Rashdall reports that the Tennysons "came in [the] Ev[enin]g to a barrel of oysters, wh[ich] they nearly emptied." [45] And on Monday, December 30, as Henry Hallam wrote to say that Arthur's body had arrived in England,[46] Rashdall met Alfred and Mary at a dinner given by the Rawnsleys. There was dancing, and Rashdall says that he did not get home till one in the morning. Tennyson stayed the night with Rawnsley and spent the next day—the last of a mournful year—talking and smoking with Rashdall and his host. "Pleasant converse," comments Rashdall, "and windy walk." [47]

On January 2 of the new year, Tennyson wrote Rashdall to say that their friend Tennant was at Somersby and asked Rashdall to come on the morrow to meet him. Rashdall's entry for the 3rd—the day Hallam was buried at Clevedon Church—is short but informative: "Rose 12. rode to Somersby, met Tennant: sat up till 3." [48] We should not of course imagine that Tennyson was lighthearted. More nearly accurate would be Tennant's judgment, probably written just at this time: "Alfred although much broken in spirits is yet able to divert his thoughts from gloomy brooding, and keep his mind in activity." [49]

On January 14, Tennyson came to Rashdall for a three-day visit, and we have a touching glimpse of him, still very much marked by sorrow, emerging chastened and sweetened from his earlier bitter mood: "A.T. improves greatly," Rashdall writes after his departure; "has evidently a mind yearning for fellowship; for the joys of friendship and love. Hallam seems to have left his heart a widowed one." [50] Rashdall's comment strikingly parallels the penultimate stanza of *In Memoriam*, LXXXV:

> My heart, tho' widow'd, may not rest
> Quite in the love of what is gone,
> But seeks to beat in time with one
> That warms another living breast.

If we did not know that this particular stanza was probably not composed till much later, we might suppose that during his visit Tennyson had read Rashdall this very early elegy.[51]

In these first months of the new year Tennyson had a great deal to keep him occupied. Emily, for one thing, was still very much in need of comfort. T. H. Rawnsley, in a letter written January 27 to Tennyson's Uncle Charles, notes that "the whole family at Somersby are I believe all tolerably well with the exception of Emily whose recent loss has indeed been a severe affliction not only to her, but to all the elder ones." [52] Rashdall, too, who visited Somersby not long after (February 14), was struck by Emily's condition: "Saw Emily T.," he says; "she does not look ill, but fearfully soul sick." [53] Alfred was much concerned, also, with the deteriorating mental health of his brother Septimus, as is shown by a strong letter he wrote in mid-January urging his uncle and grandfather to arrange for immediate treatment.[54]

16

Toward the end of January Henry Hallam wrote to suggest that Alfred and other friends contribute materials for a commemorative sketch of Arthur to be prefixed to the forthcoming *Remains*. Delaying his reply for more than two weeks, Alfred wrote on February 14:

> That you intend to print some of my friend's remains . . . has given me greater pleasure than anything I have experienced for a length of time. I attempted to draw up a memoir of his life and character, but I failed to do him justice. I failed even to please myself. I could scarcely have pleased you. I hope to be able at a future period to concentrate whatever powers I may possess on the construction of some tribute to those high speculative endowments and comprehensive sympathies which I ever loved to contemplate; but at present, tho' somewhat ashamed at my own weakness, I find the object yet is too near me to permit of any very accurate delineation.[55]

Some months later, in a letter to his grandfather, Tennyson recalled, more specifically, that "at that time my heart seemed too crushed and all my energies too paralysed to permit me any compliance with [Mr. Hallam's] request, otherwise I had not been found wanting in the dearest office I could discharge to the memory of one whom I can never forget." [56] Tennyson's own description of his grief, rather stronger than that of any other witness, suggests that he kept his feelings in these early months pretty much to himself.

Quite probably his spirits fluctuated throughout the whole year. That his moods were changeable in early February, at least, is shown by a letter of Frederick's written on the 10th: "Alfred will probably publish again in the Spring but his health is very indifferent, & his spirits very variable. He too if he does not mind will be obliged when he has lost the plumage of his Imagination, to fledge it with Tobacco leaves, if he does not take to some stronger or more fatal stimulant." [57] The ominous last sentence was prompted by the distressing condition of the second brother, Charles, whom Frederick had apparently been discussing in a passage which has since been thoroughly inked over. We know from other sources, however, that Charles in early 1834 was "killing himself with laudanum." [58]

In these winter months, while he employed himself in a fixed routine of study,[59] Alfred continued making visits in the neighborhood. On February 16, he and his brother Arthur went to call on Rashdall once more, "sat up talking & smoking till past 5," [60] and stayed over till the next evening. On March 2 Rashdall reports another visit from Alfred and Charles, and on March 5 he met Alfred again at a Rawnsley dinner, the poet returning home with him to stay till the 7th. Meanwhile, Tennyson's Aunt Fanny, basing her report apparently on Rawnsley's January letter, wrote on February 28 to say that Emily was "in a very desponding state," while the rest of the Somersby family were said to "proceed in their usual course." [61] A month later, on March 26, Julia, who had just talked with Mary, stressed more than her mother the affliction of all the Tennysons: "Poor Emily is still in a very bad state of health & spirits . . . Indeed the whole of that family is in a most melancholy state." [62] On April 18, Rashdall was at Somersby, and on the 21st he spent an evening once more at the Rawnsleys in company with Alfred, Mary, and other guests. In May, however, Rashdall went, together with Frederick, to the seashore, where they stayed till June, and we hear nothing meanwhile of Alfred. On June 18, when Rashdall brought Frederick back to Somersby, he found Alfred, Charles, the Heath brothers, and the Sellwoods; "Charles and Alfred," he reports, were "very witty." [63] This brief glimpse of the poet happy in the midst of friends, together with the quickened pace of his activity during February, March, and April, testifies to his increasing ability, during the spring and early summer, to achieve a normal life.

18

Tennyson's letter to his grandfather (quoted above and written, probably, in June),[64] also suggests that he had, since winter, much recovered himself.

From this time on, Tennyson was quite active. In July he visited both the Hallams at Molesey Park and the Heaths at their home in Surrey.[65] He returned to Somersby in late July or August [66] to meet Tennant and apparently made arrangements with him for the schooling of Horatio, Alfred's unpolished young brother.[67] Then, in late September or October (as the anniversary of Arthur's death went by), he appears to have taken Emily to the Hallams for the long-awaited meeting,[68] an event which must have brought some measure of joy to both their hearts.

But Tennyson, in late 1834, had other and perhaps more important sources of joy, for just about this time he began to be attracted to his beautiful neighbors, Sophy Rawnsley and Rosa Baring. Their function in extricating him from his grief is suggested by the poem he wrote, sometime during the year, to Sophy. It runs:

> Sweet, ask me not why I am sad,
> But, when sad thoughts arise,
> Look on me, make my spirit glad
> To gaze upon thine eyes.
> For how can sorrow dwell in mine
> If they might always gaze on thine? [69]

But, as Tennyson sought to fill the emotional vacuum left by Hallam's death, he was most powerfully drawn to Rosa; and so it is interesting to know that the little birthday poem to her, dated only 1834 in Rawnsley's *Memories of the Tennysons* (p. 65), would have been presented (as appears from Rosa's birthday book) on September 23—seven days after the anniversary of Hallam's death. It is appropriate, then, that the last entry of Tennysonian relevance in Rashdall's Lincoln-shire diary should offer a momentary sight of the beautiful Rosa. On November 3, 1834, there was a farewell party at Somersby for Rosa's family, who were leaving to spend the season in London. Rashdall attended and wrote afterward in the diary: "Somersby till 4; with Barings &c: took leave of them. Rosa the prettiest & most elegant girl I ever was intimate with. I have parted from her probably for ever! she left 4 hours after for London." [70] Tennyson, it seems, was not Rosa's only admirer. Shortly afterward, Rashdall left Lincolnshire —and Rosa—for a new charge in the south, and so, regrettably, we learn no more from him.

The revised record of Tennyson's life in the year of Hallam's death is still very scanty and, since it is taken up mostly with externals, affords only occasionally a view of the inner man. There must have been throughout this whole period recurrent fits of despair, reawakenings of sorrow, private hours of deep mourning which Rashdall and the others knew nothing of and so could not record. Nevertheless, Tennyson's progress out of his grief seems on the whole rather steady and clear; and he appears much more active than has usually been supposed, less of a recluse, less absolutely crushed, less buried in his sorrow. The evidence lightens the traditional dark portrait of the sorrowing poet.

I do not mean to imply that Hallam's death was not a very great blow to Tennyson, for it was without doubt the most severe shock of his life. But the facts seem to indicate that during 1834 Tennyson largely recovered from that shock and was addressing himself once more to life. During the year he had managed to write or draft an unusual number of very fine poems, among them "The Two Voices," "Ulysses," "Tithonus," "Morte d'Arthur," some of the *In Memoriam* elegies, and "O that 'twere possible." [71] He had been keeping in touch with his friends by letter and visit; he had, so far as we know, made no definite decision not to publish again.[72] But from the spring of 1835 till 1838, on the other hand, his poetic output seems to have been very slight, and his letters and visits cease.[73] Was this sudden slump a delayed effect of Hallam's death? Undoubtedly, in part, it was, for the loss had left him weak and vulnerable. But the relapse becomes fully intelligible only when we take into account those other developments, mentioned at the outset, which, following Hallam's death, finished the work it had begun. Among these were the psychological illness of Alfred's brothers, the uncertainty of the family's residence and future, and the final removal from Somersby in 1837. But two other developments, both directly relevant to *Maud*, were more important. The first was the death of Tennyson's grandfather in 1835 and the publication of his will, an event which ended Alfred's hopes of a comfortable independence and a settled establishment in his life and in his career as a poet. The second development was Tennyson's involvement with Rosa Baring which, promising joy, brought him, I believe, disappointment and emotional confusion. The affair was the first of three successive attachments by which he sought an effective substitute for Arthur Hallam. Since all of these are eventually relevant to *Maud* and since all are to some extent obscure, they must each be reconstructed in detail.

2

Rosa Baring

SUCH KNOWLEDGE as we have of Tennyson's relationship with Rosa Baring derives largely from a discreet and perhaps disingenuous account written sixty years ago by H. D. Rawnsley. Rawnsley was so cautious, indeed, that for half a century no writer on Tennyson ever supposed that the affair had been in any way important.[1] But in 1949 the poet's grandson, Sir Charles, taking careful note of several poems Tennyson had addressed to Rosa, went beyond Rawnsley to call the affair "serious" and to say that it had probably been discouraged by Rosa's parents.[2] Five years later, revising his opinion, Sir Charles spoke of the frustration of the affair as a "more serious blow to [Tennyson] than I had at first imagined," and was inclined to read "Locksley Hall Sixty Years After," and presumably the original "Locksley Hall," as sublimations of that frustration.[3] I have come to share Sir Charles' conclusions and to believe, in fact, that Tennyson's love for Rosa was one of the most important episodes of his life, leaving its mark not only on the "Locksley Hall" poems but on other major works as well. The complex and largely circumstantial evidence which supports this judgment will be the substance of the present chapter.

Rosa Baring was a member by birth of a very eminent commercial family. Her grandfather, Sir Francis

Baring, Bt., was chairman of the East India Company and founder of the great financial house of Baring; at his death he left a fortune of more than two million pounds and was remembered in the *Gentleman's Magazine* as "unquestionably the first merchant in Europe; first in knowledge and talents, and first in character and opulence." [4] Rosa's uncle, Alexander Baring, in 1835 was created Baron Ashburton (his daughter-in-law, the famous Lady Harriet, was later to entertain Tennyson), and cousins of hers were to become Lord Northbrook, Lord Revelstoke, and Earl of Cromer. Her father, William Baring, was Sir Francis' fourth son. Though he seems never to have been a partner in the family business,[5] William Baring was able, with his father's help, to win a fortune in India, and, when Sir Francis died in 1810, the younger Baring found himself established in what the *Gentleman's Magazine* described as "splendid independence"; he married in the same year and entered Parliament. Later he leased Lulworth Castle in Dorset (earlier the home of Mrs. Fitzherbert and afterward of Sir Robert Peel and the Duke of Gloucester) [6] and settled down to the life of a country gentleman. Unfortunately his life was not to be long, for in July, 1820, as he was rowing with a friend in the waters off the castle, the boat upset and he was drowned in full sight of his wife and friends, who were watching from the shore.[7]

Frances Baring, his widow (daughter of J. B. Poulett Thomson, an eminent merchant, and sister of Lord Sydenham, Governor-General of Canada) [8] married, in 1824, Arthur Eden, like her previous husband a younger member of a wealthy and influential family.[9] Eden was the grandson of Sir Robert Eden, Bt., a nephew of the first Lord Auckland (who took Eden under his protection upon the premature death of his father),[10] and brother-in-law of Lord Brougham. Arthur's brother Henry, with whom he has sometimes been confused,[11] rose to be an admiral, his brother John to be a general.

Arthur himself became Assistant Comptroller of the Exchequer, a post he held until his retirement in 1851.[12] In 1825 or thereabouts he leased Harrington Hall, a beautiful brick manor house about two miles from Somersby Rectory.[13] There, while he and his wife took a full and even a leading part in the social activities of the neighborhood,[14] their children grew up in friendship with the Tennysons, the Rawnsleys, and the Massingberds.[15]

We get some significant impressions of the family from the diaries of two neighboring clergymen—John Rashdall and Francis Charles Massingberd (rector of Ormsby and future Chancellor of Lincoln), who in 1839 married Fanny Baring, Rosa's sister. Rashdall found Arthur Eden "very intelligent," "very agreeable," with "all the urbanity of [a] high bred gentleman." But his conversation, on at least one occasion, "was entirely on Sporting," which, Rashdall said, was "not in my way." [16] Massingberd took a dimmer view of the worldly Eden. He found to his distress that "all her [Fanny's] family [were] irreligious," and he objected very much to their card-playing ("Mem: Record now my solemn protest against myself if I ever permit it at my house. Sure to be tried, and yᵉ trial is a *severe* one to my love of approbation and delight in giving pleasure—But if *once* admitted, it will be wanted always"). Massingberd, as we see from this, was something of a prig, and his fiancée's family were consequently somewhat cold toward him. He reported late in his courtship that he was "very much mortified to find that her family, especially her Father in law seem so little cordial. After all their assurances, it seems very unjust." [17]

Charlotte-Rose Baring, her father's youngest daughter, was born probably between the years 1812 and 1814, so that she was about five years younger than Tennyson.[18] They would have known each other for approximately two years before the poet went up to Cambridge in 1827 and would have met only during his vacations until, after his father's death in 1831, Tennyson returned without a degree to take up steady residence at Somersby. Rosa, as she was called, was an unusually pretty woman, "the prettiest and most elegant girl," said Rashdall, with whom he had ever been intimately acquainted; and Rosa's portrait has survived to vindicate Rashdall's judgment.[19] In addition to beauty she undoubtedly had wealth—from her father and probably from her mother also. One imagines that with such qualifications she was not without eligible suitors. Illuminating in this respect are some verses sent her on her golden wedding anniversary by her friend (and Tennyson's) Sophy Rawnsley Elmhirst, who had been her bridesmaid:

> I well remember how thy spouse
> No little envy did arouse;
> For all men felt the "prize" were gone,
> And they, poor dupes, were left forlorn.
>
> But wounds like those are skin-deep, sure;
> What men can't cure, they must endure;
> So with good grace they now confess,
> "Another" thou wert born to bless.[20]

The man whose triumph is thus so lamely celebrated was Robert Duncombe Shafto, grandson of the "Bobby Shafto" long familiar to children,[21] scion of a wealthy old Durham family and a first cousin of Arthur Eden, with whose family the Shaftoes had been closely connected for three generations.[22] The marriage, an excellent and obvious match of which more will be said later, took place on October 22, 1838.

Nothing preserved in the Shafto family greatly illuminates Rosa's relationship with Tennyson, since all diaries and letters from her early years have disappeared. A number of travel diaries from later life tell only that Rosa was a thoroughly ordinary gentlewoman —complacent, slightly vain, and not at all inclined to introspection or reflection—who took life pretty much

25

as it came, finding little to record except her times of rising and dining and the rounds of sights and visits. She seems, nevertheless, to have been a woman of considerable energy, for she sometimes complains of the lack of it in those about her; and she was, to judge by the diaries and family tradition, very gay, very fond of clothes and company, and a bit inclined to extravagance. Besides these diaries nothing remains except Rosa's birthday book, a present from her husband, in which are preserved the autographs of Tennyson's verses to her which Rawnsley printed in his *Memories*. Other poems, some by Tennyson, some by other poets, have been copied into the book, but except for Mrs. Elmhirst's lines of congratulation, only one of these is of any interest. This is a short poem written in 1885 by one G. Blunt—apparently a friend of Mrs. Shafto's —whose reflections were prompted by Tennyson's verses and, perhaps, by Rosa's reminiscences:

> Long years have passed since he whose Art
> Filled life with poetry to the brim,
> Praised from a youthful burning heart
> The Rose of all the world to him.
> All things have changed & in our Eyes
> Both heaven & Earth seem growing cold,
> The dawn no longer fills the skies,
> No roses bloom like those of old—
> Alas! t'is [sic] we not they who change;
> This world for us is not for aye;
> Yet Roses bloom beyond its range,
> And light and love can never die.

The lines seem to suggest that Rosa thought of Tennyson's attachment as a strong one or was at least willing to let others think so. But family tradition has preserved nothing in this respect except the fact that she was, in youth, Tennyson's friend.

We are consequently thrown back, for knowledge of the relationship, to more tenuous evidence. The only direct account of the affair is Rawnsley's, and Rawns-

ley, as I have said, does not incline one to believe that
the attachment was very serious. He had his information, he tells us, directly from Rosa, whom he "only
knew as a sweet old lady"; [23] but his father, his grandfather, and his aunt had known Tennyson and Rosa
very well in those early Lincolnshire days and after,[24]
so that he had other possible sources of information as
well. But how much he knew, and how much he told
of what he knew, must remain obscure, although, as I
indicate below, there is some reason to believe that
he thought more than he wrote. Rawnsley gives us
three poems written by Tennyson to Rosa, and he
transmits from her some rather gushing reminiscences,
which, though they do not tell us very much, certainly
deserve quotation:

> Often would she speak of the way in which she
> and her companions round Somersby, who were
> not too frightened of him, hung upon the words
> of the quaint, shy, long-haired young man, who
> had in his boyhood's day made an impression of
> being more learned and more thoughtful than was
> common, and seemed wise beyond his years. She
> would tell of how she and one of her girl friends,
> in admiration of the young poet, would ride over
> to Somersby, just to have the pleasure of pleasing
> him or teasing him as the case might be. From
> time to time he would write a verse or two for one
> or other of the girls who had been with him at
> a picnic in the woods, or send some little verse of
> reconciliation after a tiff at a dance; and although
> she confessed that all poetry in those days seemed
> to her mere "jangledom," yet it was always de-
> lightful to her to believe that the "rose of the rose-
> bud garden of girls," had reference to her. "Alfred,
> as we all called him, was so quaint and so chiv-
> alrous, such a real knight among men, at least I
> always fancied so; and though we joked one an-
> other about his quaint, taciturn ways, which were

27

mingled strangely with boisterous fits of fun, we were proud as peacocks to have been worthy of notice by him, and treasured any message he might send or any word of admiration he let fall." [25]

Nothing in these rather sugary recollections indicates that the attachment was serious on either side, or even, indeed, that there was an attachment. But between Rosa and her memories of the strange, unkempt, pipe-smoking poet who was so taciturn and quaint lay fifty years during which Tennyson had become Laureate, a peer of the realm, and one of the most famous literary figures of his time; and between Rosa's words and us intervenes the reverential Rawnsley, disinclined in himself to retail impious anecdotes of the great bard and very much aware of the primly censorious temper of his friend Hallam, second Lord Tennyson, who had found no occasion in his *Memoir* to mention Rosa at all. We do not wonder, then, that Rawnsley should speak of "sisterly affection," despite the contradictory evidence of the following poem, which, somewhat para-doxically, he quotes with the remark that it was ad-dressed to Rosa after a "lover's quarrel" at a ball:

To Rosa, 1836

Sole rose of beauty, loveliness complete,
If those few words were bitter or unjust,
Yet is thy gentle nature so discreet
That they will pass thee like an idle gust.
Henceforward, fancy shall not force distrust,
But all my blood in time to thine shall beat,
Henceforth I lay my pride within the dust
And my whole heart is vassal at thy feet.
Blow, summer rose, thy beauty makes me
    shamed
That I could blame thee! Heaven's dewdrop
    pure
Bathe, with my tears, thy maiden blossom
    sweet:

28

Blow, summer rose, nor fall; and, oh, be sure
That if I had not loved, I had not blamed;
For my whole heart is vassal at thy feet.

By all my grief for that which I did say,
By all the life of love that never dies,
By all that Paradise for which we pray
And all the Paradise that round thee lies,
By thoughts of thee that like the Heavens rise,
Star after star, within me, day by day,
And night by night, in musing on thine eyes,
Which look me through when thou art far
    away,
By that madonna grace of parted hair
And dewy sister eyelids drooping chaste,
By each dear foot, so light on field, or floor,
By that full form and slender moulded waist,
And that all perfect smile of thine, I swear,
That these rash lips shall blame thee, Rose,
    no more.[26]

The feeling in this poem is obviously not brotherly affection but infatuation manifestly sincere and fervent. Naïve, idealistic, almost painfully reticent, Tennyson was not likely at any time to voice such sentiments without genuine involvement, but he was when he wrote this poem not a boy in love with love but a man of twenty-six who only two years before had been shattered by the death of Arthur Hallam. Spiritually adrift as he was, he would have had little inclination for trifling flirtations but must rather have been seeking to redirect the emotional energies which, once absorbed in Hallam, were now without a living object. His involvement with Rosa, therefore, may well have been a more serious matter than Rawnsley was willing to allow.

"To Rosa" is only one of a number of poems addressed to her by Tennyson which have survived to give us some degree of insight into the nature and development of his attraction to her. But it may be that the earliest traces of the affair are to be found not in these poems but (with a considerable increment of fiction) in "The Gardener's Daughter," a poem in which Sir Charles has seen significant autobiographical implications:

> [In the summer of 1833 Tennyson and Arthur Hallam] spent many happy weeks together at the old Rectory—weeks which Alfred was to remember with piercing regret during the sixty years of life that remained to him. The spirit of them lives in *The Gardener's Daughter,* which was composed at that time. . . . This mood was, I think, largely due to a great emotional development which the poet had undergone during the past eighteen months. The eroticism of *The Gardener's Daughter,* though reticent according to modern standards, has a keener edge and a greater directness than any of Tennyson's earlier writings, and these qualities are even more apparent in the early drafts of the poem. No doubt Arthur's engagement to Emily, though it had not in any sense weakened the friendship between him and Alfred, had served to release in his friend emotions, which the exclusiveness of their early affection had tended to absorb.[27]

The biographical situation described here is directly reflected in the poem. The friendship of the speaker and Eustace—"a friendship so complete / Portion'd in halves between us, that we grew / The fable of the city where we dwelt"—is clearly the poetic counterpart of Alfred's friendship for Hallam, just as Eustace's engagement to Juliet finds its analogue in Hallam's engagement to Emily Tennyson. What then is to be said of the rapturous attachment which the speaker, in emulation of Eustace, forms for "Rose, the Gardener's Daughter"? Tennyson could hardly have used the name without thinking of his beautiful neighbor, whom he had certainly known for years, and of the literal garden of "Eden where she dwelt" which was later (we shall see) to form so special a part of his memories of her. The poetic Rose, furthermore, shares with the real one her glossy brown hair, her violet eyes, and her full bosom, and she is extensively associated with the flower for which she is named, just as Rosa is associated in the poems Tennyson shortly was to write to or about her. These likenesses suggest that the opening portrait of Rose in the poem was intended as an oblique compliment to Rosa, even though the details of the love story can hardly express more than Tennyson's hopeful extrapolation of his incipient passion.

Such a reading of "The Gardener's Daughter" is supported by the fact that in the fall of 1834, not long after he had finished that poem, his feeling for Rosa manifested itself in the first of the poems which in the next two years he was to write to or about her:

Thy rosy lips are soft and sweet,
Thy fairy form is so complete,
Thy motions are so airy free,
Love lays his armour at thy feet
And yields his bow to thee;
Take any dart from out his quiver
And pierce what heart thou wilt for ever.[28]

This pretty offer of the poet's heart is too conventional to allow us to see very deeply into the state of mind which lay behind it; more indicative of his early feelings, perhaps, are two poems of which Rosa had no copy. The first of these Tennyson recited in 1854 to F. T. Palgrave: [29]

June on many a flower reposes,
Many a blossom May discloses,
    But in Autumn unto me
Blooms a rose, the rose of roses.

Rose of roses, bliss of blisses,
Rosebud-lips for honey-kisses;

East & West & North & South
Bear not such a rose as this is.

Perfect world of winning graces,
Music-made for Love's embraces,
    Many a face I see, but thine
Sweeter than all human faces.

Rose of roses, bliss of blisses,
What care I for other's kisses?
    When a thousand years are dead
Comes there no such rose as this is.

Love & fancy shape caresses,
Twenty million tendernesses;
    All my life & heart & soul
Tangle in her shining tresses.

Rose of roses, bliss of blisses,
Were not thine the kiss of kisses?
    Ah! for such a kiss as that!
    Ah! for such a rose as this is.

Although Palgrave, perhaps at Tennyson's direction, has entitled these lines "Early Verses of Compliment to Miss Rose Baring," they are clearly more than that, expressing as they do a genuine if somewhat boyish mood of infatuation. There is no way of determining when they were written, but their style and feeling seem to link them with the 1834 verses just quoted and the early stages of Tennyson's attachment.

"The Rosebud," a short poem written probably in 1834, must, I think, also refer to Rosa:

    The night with sudden odour reel'd,
    The southern stars a music peal'd,
    Warm beams across the meadow stole;
    For Love flew over grove and field,
    Said, "Open Rosebud, open, yield
        Thy fragrant soul." [30]

This published version of the poem omits the first line of the manuscript, in which the speaker describes himself kneeling in flowers, but even with it the poem remains obscure, a tantalizingly cryptic record of a moment of feeling whose context we are left to guess. But whether the lines recall merely an instant of passionate longing or are associated in some way with the memory of a prospective tryst, they are a remarkable evocation in strikingly concrete and vivid terms of the intensity which Tennyson's infatuation achieved.

"To Rosa," quoted earlier and written in 1835 or 1836,[31] offers a more sharply focused view of the affair. In the 1834 birthday verses and the "Verses of Compliment" Tennyson appears to worship from afar; now he assumes the right to be jealous, openly and directly avows his love, and seems even in his vassalage to presume somewhat on Rosa's response. It is therefore difficult to imagine that there had not, previous to the "lovers' quarrel," been a partial understanding between them, so that the poem presupposes at least a measure of involvement on Rosa's part, something which the earlier poems leave in doubt. The poem also shows a deep tinge of the idealized erotic feeling manifested in "The Rosebud" and a stronger and more particularized sense of Rosa's physical beauty than either of the other two early poems.

Tennyson left one other record of the strength his feeling attained, in a poem not written in the impetuosity of young manhood but, remarkably enough, more than fifty years afterward, when, one would have supposed, the memory of his early love had long ago passed away. "Roses on the Terrace," published in 1889, may have been written when Tennyson, convalescing from a very serious illness, heard in March the news of Robert Shafto's death [32]—or perhaps at some time during the previous few years. Tennyson has obscured the reference of the poem slightly by compounding the terrace of his home at Aldworth, which looked out over a wide expanse of the Sussex weald to the blue line of downs bounding the sea, with the terraced garden at Harrington Hall, where the incident alluded to must have taken place:

> Rose, on this terrace fifty years ago,
>> When I was in my June, you in your May,
> Two words, "*My* Rose," set all your face aglow,
>> And now that I am white, and you are gray,
> That blush of fifty years ago, my dear,
>> Blooms in the Past, but close to me to-day
> As this red rose, which on our terrace here
>> Glows in the blue of fifty miles away.

Just what besides a blush followed his declaration, Tennyson does not say, but we may well imagine that it was no insignificant moment which came flooding back upon the old poet then so close to death.[33] The poem suggests more strongly than any of the contemporary pieces the strength of Tennyson's feeling, and it seems to indicate that Rosa to some extent returned his feeling and that the feelings of both found at least a momentary *éclaircissement*.

But whatever happened in that long-remembered interview, other poems show that the affair fell upon harder times. Two sonnets printed by Sir Charles in *Unpublished Early Poems* tell the story of a love moving by stages into disillusionment. The first seems to have been written during a rainy Lincolnshire fall (in 1835 or 1836) when Rosa was going up to London for the season with her family.

> Ah, fade not yet from out the green arcades,
>> Fade not, sweet Rose, for hark! the wood-
>>> land shrills,
> A lamentation grows in all the shades,
>> And grief in copses where the linnet trills:
>> The sweet Rose fades from all the winding
>>> rills
> And waning arches of the golden glades:
>> From all the circuit of the purple hills

> The sweet Rose fades, alas, how soon it fades.
> It does not fade, but from the land it goes,
>> And leaves the land to winter. I remain,
>>> To waste alone the slowly-narrowing
>>> days.
> It fades to me: for they transplant the Rose,
>> And further South the Rose will bloom
>> again,
>>> Like a mere Rose that only cares for
>>> praise.

The hint of disappointment in the last line suggests that Rosa had become more indifferent to him than he would have liked, a development even more apparent in the second of the sonnets.

> I lingered yet awhile to bend my way
>> To that far South, for which my spirits ache,
> For under rainy hills a jewel lay
>> And this dark land was precious for its sake,
>> A rosy-coloured jewel, fit to make
> An emperor's signet-ring, to save or slay
>> Whole peoples, such as some great King
>> might take
> To clasp his mantle on a festal day:
> And yet a jewel only made to shine,
>> And icy cold although 'tis rosy clear—
>>> Why did I linger? I myself condemn,
> For ah! 'tis far too costly to be mine,
>> And nature never dropt a human tear
>>> In those chill dews whereof she froze the
>>> gem.[34]

"Far too costly to be mine"—the phrase indicates clearly enough the barrier of wealth between them which must from the first have doomed the affair to failure, even had Rosa been less indifferent than these verses seem to say she was.

The two sonnets just discussed belong, on the evidence of manuscript watermarks, to the period 1835–1836,[35] so that the affair may very well have been at an end when, in May, 1836, Tennyson addressed the "Bridesmaid" sonnet to Emily Sellwood.[36] It is an interesting fact that "I lingered yet awhile" is preserved on one of two conjugate leaves, with the "Bridesmaid" sonnet (see pp. 67–68, below) facing it on the opposite leaf, while on the reverse appears a poem which has, in this context, interesting implications:

> How thought you that this thing could cap-
>> tivate?
>> What are those graces that could make her
>>> dear,
>> Who is not worth the notice of a sneer
> To rouse the vapid devil of her hate?
> A speech conventional, so void of weight
>> That after it has buzzed about one's ear,
>> 'Twere rich refreshment for a week to hear
> The dentist babble or the barber prate;
> A hand displayed with many a little art;
>> An eye that glances on her neighbour's
>>> dress;
>> A foot too often shewn for my regard;
> An angel's form—a waiting-woman's heart;
>> A perfect-featured face, expressionless,
>>> Insipid, as the Queen upon a card.[37]

Such poems are not written gratuitously. It may be that this bitter little sonnet records the last stage of Tennyson's disillusionment with Rosa, before he turned away from her to Emily Sellwood. (The same mood may also have found more moderate expression in the published poem, "The form, the form alone is eloquent.") [38] But though the four sonnets thus arranged do seem to make a rather neat chronological pattern, we cannot finally be sure in what order they were written, since no evidence allows us to say how quickly Tennyson's feeling for Emily developed or how completely it may have obliterated his feeling for Rosa. Since he seems to have written still another (though perhaps significantly subdued) poem to Rosa in September, 1836,[39] it is possible if not probable that the sonnets of disillusionment post-date the beginnings of his attraction to Emily and that the two affairs cannot be so neatly separated in time.

At this point all direct evidence of Tennyson's attachment to Rosa ends, and we are left to make what sense we can of the rather scanty materials so far presented. In these half-dozen poems we see a dim shape in the relationship as it grows from a more or less conventional romantic involvement to serious passion and finally to disillusionment; and we can see that, at the end of the affair at least, Rosa's feeling was not strong enough to oppose whatever discouragement her parents may have offered to Tennyson's suit. And considering the social and economic position of Rosa's family and the unhappy history of Tennyson's, together with Alfred's poverty, strange appearance, and unconventional habits,[40] we may well imagine with Sir Charles, that Arthur Eden and his wife would not have been inclined to give him much encouragement. But correspondence and other contemporary records of Tennyson's life in the crucial years 1835–1837 are almost completely lacking, and the poems alone do not allow us to estimate with any accuracy what the precise course of the affair was, what parts the various participants played, and what in particular brought the affair to an end—or how, and with what result. We might guess from "Roses on the Terrace" that the romance left Tennyson with an enduring psychic mark, but it is only when we turn to the indirect and admittedly tenuous evidence of certain of Tennyson's published poems that we can begin to comprehend what those effects were and something, perhaps, of the causes which produced them.

From their first publication to the present day, "Locksley Hall" and *Maud* have persistently aroused the suspicion that they were in some sense autobiographical. In 1847, for instance, George Gilfillan described "Locksley Hall" as telling "a tale of unfortunate passion with a gusto and depth of feeling, which (unless we misconstrue the mark of the branding iron) betray more than a fictitious interest in the theme." [41] And in 1960, as we shall see, the author of a late study of Tennyson voices a similar opinion. The reasons for these suspicions are perfectly plain: No hint of irony, no frame of dramatic objectification qualifies in the least the extravagantly self-centered emotion of the protagonists in these poems, so that most competent commentators have seen the two as to some extent mouthpieces for Tennyson himself. This does not mean, of course, that the situations in the poems are autobiographical. Tennyson himself, indeed, vehemently denied that they were: " 'Locksley Hall' is thought by many to be an autobiographical sketch; it's nothing of the sort—not a word of my history in it"; [42] it was "a simple invention as to place, incidents, and people." [43] To a translator who had been imprudent enough to say otherwise, he wrote:

> I must object and strongly to the statement in your Preface that *I* am the hero in either poem [the two "Locksley Halls"]. I never had a cousin Amy, "Locksley Hall" is an entirely imaginative edifice. My grandsons are little boys. I am not even white headed, I never had a gray hair in my head. The whole thing is a dramatic impersonation, but I find in almost all modern criticism this absurd tendency to personalities. Some of my thought may come out into the poem, but am I therefore the hero? *There is not one touch of biography in it from beginning to end.*[44]

The statement is peculiarly literal. In another mood and speaking privately to his son, he was willing to admit that there might after all be some connection between such poems and his life:

> About "Maud" [writes Hallam Tennyson] and other monodramatic poems (the stories of which

were his own creation) he said to me: "In a certain way, no doubt, poets and novelists, however dramatic they are, give themselves in their works. The mistake that people make is that they think the poet's poems are a kind of 'catalogue raisonné' of his very own self, and of all the facts of his life, not seeing that they often only express a poetic instinct, or judgment on character real or imagined, and on the facts of lives real or imagined." [45] Students have recently come to recognize, under the influence of Sir Charles, that both "Locksley Hall" and *Maud* are in part the poetic expression of some of the facts of Tennyson's early life, particularly of the feud between the two branches of the Tennyson family.[46] Not much attention, however, has been paid to the central situation in both poems, which involves the love of a high-strung, idealistic young man, brooding and inclined to morbidity, for a young woman of wealth and position, and the frustration of that love through the snobbish opposition of the girl's family. Nor has anyone attempted to explain why Tennyson was so absorbed with this particular story that he told it, with variations, three more times: in "Edwin Morris," in "Pelleas and Ettarre," and in "Aylmer's Field," not to mention the sequel of "Locksley Hall." "Aylmer's Field," of course, was based on an account given him by Thomas Woolner,[47] a fact which reminds us that the story in these poems is not in itself uncommon; what is uncommon is the frequency and the passion with which Tennyson told it. Hallam Tennyson writes of "Aylmer's Field":

> The opening lines . . . unfold the moral of that poem. The sequel describes the Nemesis which fell upon Sir Aylmer Aylmer in his pride of wealth. My father always felt a prophet's righteous wrath against this form of selfishness; and no one can read his terrible denunciations of such pride

trampling on a holy human love, without being aware that the poet's heart burnt within him while at work on this tale of wrong.[48]

What fact of life, real or imagined, generated that "prophet's righteous wrath," and directed it, in this poem and the others, against the "filthy marriage-hindering Mammon"?

Jerome H. Buckley, struck like so many readers before him by the excessive self-pity with which the hero of "Locksley Hall" views himself and the excessive jealousy with which he views his faithless Amy and her prospective husband, has recently concluded that the poem may in part reflect Tennyson's disappointment at the breaking off in 1840 of his correspondence with Emily Sellwood; and he is therefore inclined to adopt W. D. Templeman's view that "Locksley Hall" was written in 1840–1841, even though, as he admits, "it seems unlikely . . . that the faithless Amy of the poem . . . could in any respect represent Emily Sellwood, who in any case was not forced into a marriage of convenience with a drunken clown." [49] It would indeed be difficult to see Emily Sellwood in Amy; so that if one is inclined, as I for one am, to agree with Professor Buckley's feeling that the poem owes something to Tennyson's "personal experience of sundered love," we must look elsewhere for the experience.

The trouble lies in assigning the poem to so late a date as 1841. Professor Templeman bases his argument for that date, first, on his thesis that the poem shows the influence of Carlyle's *Sartor Resartus;* and secondly, on a report by J. C. Walters of a tradition that Tennyson wrote the poem at North Somercotes during a period of six weeks which Templeman rather arbitrarily associates with the weeks Tennyson is recorded to have spent in 1841 at Mablethorpe.[50] But, as Templeman says, Tennyson could have read *Sartor* any time from 1834 on; and since the poet loved the Lincolnshire coast and visited it often both before and after he left

Lincolnshire, there is no reason (supposing Walter's unconfirmed tradition to be correct) to single out the Mablethorpe visit of 1841 as identical with a North Somercotes visit in an unknown year. Several pieces of evidence, on the other hand, argue for an earlier date: (1) the sole manuscript of the poem is watermarked "1835," which, though it does not prove that the poem was written in that year, tells against a date so late as 1841; [51] (2) the *Memoir* records that Tennyson took the "hungry lion" image in the poem from Thomas Pringle's *Narrative of a Residence in South Africa,* which he read in 1837; [52] (3) Edmund Lushington records an (uncertain) recollection that in 1837 or early 1838 he heard Tennyson read "Locksley Hall" in his London chambers; [53] and (4) Hallam Tennyson associates the line describing "The light of London flaring like a dreary dawn" with Tennyson's residence at High Beech, which began probably in November of 1837. [54] These facts together seem to point to a date for the poem of late 1837 or, more probably, 1838. If we make the likely assumption, with Professor Templeman, that the poem was written in Lincolnshire, we might wish to place its composition in the spring of 1838, when Tennyson returned there for a visit. [55] Or, if we agree also with Templeman's view that the poem was influenced by *Sartor Resartus,* which was published in book form in July, 1838, [56] we may place the composition, if we wish, during Tennyson's Mablethorpe visit of 1839 [57] or during some unrecorded visit of the previous summer or fall.

But if "Locksley Hall" was written in 1837 or 1838, it is obvious from what personal experience of sundered love it may derive. Tennyson had then very recently been in love with Rosa Baring, if indeed the embers of his feeling were not still smouldering; and certainly, sensitive and inclined to nourish psychic wounds as he was, he may have felt a surge of jealousy when, just before his departure from Somersby in November, 1837,

41

he heard rumors of Rosa's engagement to Shafto.[58] He would have left Lincolnshire feeling more or less acutely the pangs of despised love, together with the accumulated burden of other painful memories of the troubles with his uncle's family. In the year that followed, as his son tells us, in new surroundings and secure in his quasi-engagement to Emily, Tennyson experienced a liberating infusion of a new positive spirit;[59] but that spirit must have developed slowly, over a period of some months. Returning to Lincolnshire on the visits of the ensuing year (and hearing definite news of Rosa's engagement and approaching marriage),[60] he must still have felt the oppression of the past and a need to free himself from it. His hero's gesture of liberation from the fickle girl, the Hall, and the uncle who had caused him so much pain, was a gesture which Tennyson himself must have been very much in a mood to make. For him in 1838, as for his hero, the poem would have marked a spiritual turning point—a conscious, retrospective break with the past and a hopeful prophecy of a fuller future. Placed at this point in his development, as all the evidence encourages us to place it, the poem, so clearly corresponding to his own situation, is pregnant with biographical meaning.

This association of "Locksley Hall" with Tennyson's life is strengthened by the fact that the marriage of Shafto and Rosa was a marriage of arrangement; for Rosa's step-aunt, Lady Brougham, writes in her diary under January 2, 1838: "Robert Shafto went away [from London] . . . I saw plainly he had not made up his mind to marry Rosa Baring as they wished & did not wish to bring the matter to a conclusion."[61] Lady Brougham is not often very informative, but she tells us here (in addition to the fact that the rumors of engagement were premature) that the marriage was the result, not primarily of Shafto's romantic attraction to Rosa, nor presumably of hers to him, but of the desire of her parents for a match suitable to their financial circumstances and family background; it was a marriage, in short, like Amy's to her squire, arranged by parents for social and economic reasons. It is not hard to imagine how Tennyson would have felt about such a transaction:

> Cursed be the social wants that sin against
> the strength of youth!
> Cursed be the social lies that warp us from
> the living truth!
>
> Cursed be the sickly forms that err from hon-
> est Nature's rule!
> Cursed be the gold that gilds the straiten'd
> forehead of the fool! . . .
>
> What is that which I should turn to, lighting
> upon days like these?
> Every door is barr'd with gold, and opens but
> to golden keys.

Or how he would have felt about Rosa:

> O my cousin, shallow-hearted! O my Amy,
> mine no more!
> O the dreary, dreary moorland! O the barren,
> barren shore!
>
> Falser than all fancy fathoms, falser than all
> songs have sung,
> Puppet to a father's threat, and servile to a
> shrewish tongue!
>
> Is it well to wish thee happy?—having
> known me—to decline
> On a range of lower feelings and a narrower
> heart than mine!

Or toward Duncombe Shafto:

> As the husband is, the wife is: thou art mated
> with a clown,

And the grossness of his nature will have
    weight to drag thee down.

He will hold thee, when his passion shall
    have spent its novel force,
Something better than his dog, a little dearer
    than his horse.

What is this? his eyes are heavy; think not
    they are glazed with wine.
Go to him, it is thy duty; kiss him, take his
    hand in thine.

Duncombe Shafto was no drunken brute, but he was
apparently a worldly man, fond of cards and the hunt;
in the eyes of the high-minded young Tennyson,
blurred by jealousy, he might have looked something
like this caricature of the coarse Victorian husband, especially when the dramatic personality the poet had
assumed released him from any responsibility for his
judgment. He came much closer to an accurate description of Shafto fifty years later:

Worthier soul was he than I am, sound and
    honest, rustic Squire,
Kindly landlord, boon companion—youthful
    jealousy is a liar.

Duncombe Shafto was too cosmopolitan to be called
a rustic, but—justice of the peace, member of Parliament, large landholder—he otherwise fits very well
into the outlines of the portrait.[62]

In "Locksley Hall Sixty Years After," as Sir Charles
Tennyson has pointed out,[63] we have Tennyson's poetical sublimation of much of the emotional burden of
his life: the poem expresses, in the old speaker's lament
for his sailor son, Tennyson's sharp grief for his
own dear son Lionel, recently dead;[64] it offers a tribute, in the portrait of Edith, to the Emily Sellwood who in her spiritual ministrations had rescued
him from his earlier morbid estrangement from the
world:

> Very woman of very woman, nurse of ailing
>   body and mind,
> She that link'd again the broken chain that
>   bound me to my kind.[65]

It voices, likewise, perhaps, his sense of spiritual reconciliation with his once-hated grandfather, the "Old Man of the Wolds":

> Gone the tyrant of my youth, and mute below the chancel stones,
> All his virtues—I forgive them—black in white above his bones.

But if these correspondences hold good, what can be said of the speaker's recollections of Amy? Does not the old man remember her in relation to Edith very much as Tennyson must have remembered Rosa in relation to Emily?

> Amy loved me, Amy fail'd me, Amy was a
>   timid child . . .

> Here to-day was Amy with me, while I wander'd down the coast,
> Near us Edith's holy shadow, smiling at the slighter ghost.

"Here today was Amy with me," very much as, sometime in the next three years, Rosa was to be with Tennyson in his Aldworth garden. Is it not remarkable that Tennyson should, in "Roses on the Terrace," remember a moment with Rosa so very much like the moment when the speaker in the first "Locksley Hall" declared his love to Amy?

> Rose, on this terrace fifty years ago,
>   When I was in my June, you in your May,
> Two words, "*My* Rose," set all your face
>   aglow,
>   And now that I am white and you are gray,
> That blush of fifty years ago, my dear,
>   Blooms in the Past, but close to me to-day,
> As this red rose, which on our terrace here
>   Glows in the blue of fifty miles away.

45

And I said, "My cousin Amy, speak, and
    speak the truth to me,
Trust me, cousin, all the current of my being
    sets to thee."

On her pallid cheek and forehead came a
    colour and a light,
As I have seen the rosy red flushing in the
    northern night.

I was struck long ago by the fact that in each of these poems of defeated love the residence of the heroine should loom so curiously large in the imagination of the hero, and I began very early to suspect that these mansions were associated in Tennyson's memory with Harrington Hall, the symbol to him, as the imaginary buildings are to his heroes, at once of her status and her inaccessibility. But obviously what is preserved in the poetic Locksley Hall, if I am correct, is not the exact reproduction of an original that Victorian source-hunters looked for so assiduously, but an edifice which could function in Tennyson's imagination as a psychological equivalent of Harrington. His description of the Hall in the original poem is indeed very vague; it is a hall overlooking some sandy tracts on a (Lincolnshire) seacoast and so resembles Harrington in nothing but the fact that it is a hall. Nevertheless, in the sequel Tennyson furnished Locksley Hall with a "gateway tower" vaguely reminiscent of the central tower which is the distinctive feature of Harrington and, more significantly, with a chapel, "slowly sinking now into the ground," where "lies the warrior, my forefather, with his feet upon the hound. / Cross'd." In Harrington chapel there is a figure of a crusader with his feet crossed upon a small lion, held by tradition to be a representation of Sir John Harrington, founder of the house of Harrington as the figure in the poem is the "founder of our blood." In the early nineteenth century Harrington chapel (later rebuilt) was in a bad state of disrepair, "slowly sinking into the ground." [66]

There is real reason to suspect, then, that the "Locksley Hall" poems owe a good deal to Tennyson's memories of Rosa. But it is only by inspecting certain other, related poems that we can apprehend fully the importance of those memories and their function in Tennyson's imagination. In 1839, probably not more than a year after he wrote "Locksley Hall," Tennyson began "Edwin Morris," [67] an amorphous poem which, opening with the speaker's recollections of his early friendship with Edwin Morris, an overelaborate poet, and the "fat-faced curate" Edward Bull, ends with the largely unrelated story of the speaker's love for Letty Hill. The Hills are, like the Edens at Harrington, "new-comers in an ancient hold" and, like the Barings and Poulett Thomsons, commercial millionaires; the ancient hold is, like Harrington, a "bulk / Of mellow brickwork." [68] The Hills' house, however, is not in Lincolnshire but on an island in one of the Llanberis lakes, in which region Tennyson wrote the poem; and the speaker is, of course, not a poet but, like the speaker of "The Gardener's Daughter," a landscape painter.

The speaker recalls that in the space of a few months his courtship of Letty withered, "nipt to death by him / That was a God, and is a lawyer's clerk, / The rentroll Cupid of our rainy isles"—in short, by her parents' objections to his lack of income. Nevertheless Letty sends a note signed " 'Your Letty, only yours,' " and the two lovers have a last clandestine meeting:

> . . . she moved,
> Like Proserpine in Enna, gathering flowers:
> Then low and sweet I whistled thrice; and she,
> She turn'd, we closed, we kiss'd, swore faith, I breathed
> In some new planet: A silent cousin stole
> Upon us and departed: "Leave," she cried,
> "O leave me!" "Never, dearest, never: here

47

I brave the worst:" and while we stood like
    fools
Embracing, all at once a score of pugs
And poodles yell'd within, and out they came
Trustees and Aunts and Uncles. "What, with
    him!
Go" (shrill'd the cotton-spinning chorus);
    "him!"
I choked. Again they shriek'd the burthen—
    "Him!"
Again with hands of wild rejection "Go!—
Girl, get you in!" She went—and in one
    month
They wedded her to sixty thousand pounds,
To lands in Kent and messuages in York,
And slight Sir Robert with his watery smile
And educated whisker.

It is a sharp and bitter little vignette, bringing to mind
in some of its details an unaccountable reference in
"Locksley Hall Sixty Years After," when the old hero
remembers, with no allusion to anything in either
"Locksley Hall," a time when Amy "shrank, and put
me from her, shriek'd, and started from my side," except that here it is the relatives who shriek and wield
"hands of wild rejection." But in this passage too there
is an inexplicable detail, the single word "Trustees,"
which is the British equivalent for "guardians." Letty
Hill is not, so far as we are told, an orphan, and nothing in the poem explains why she would need trustees.
But Rosa Baring, the daughter of a deceased and
wealthy father, would most assuredly have had trustees, who might have objected as much to Rosa's marrying a poor poet as Letty's to her marrying a poor landscape painter.[69]

"Sir Robert with his watery smile and educated
whisker" resembles the handsome, clean-shaven Robert
Shafto in nothing but his wealth and lands, although
Shafto, unlike Sir Robert with his "lands in Kent and

48

messuages in York," had his principal holdings in Durham with messuages in Wiltshire.[70] But the hero of the poem views Sir Robert with less rancor than his compeer of "Locksley Hall" feels toward his rival, and he shows also less bitterness toward Letty than the speaker of "Locksley Hall" for Amy:

> So left the place, left Edwin, nor have seen
> Him since, nor heard of her, nor cared to
>   hear.
>   Nor cared to hear? Perhaps: yet long ago
> I have pardon'd little Letty; not indeed,
> It may be, for her own dear sake but this,
> She seems a part of those fresh days to me;
> For in the dust and drouth of London life
> She moves among my visions of the lake,
> While the prime swallow dips his wing, or
>   then
> While the gold-lily blows, and overhead
> The light cloud smoulders on the summer
>   crag.

But all the middle part of this passage had found no place in Tennyson's 1839 draft, where Letty is left sardonically apostrophized as "O facile nose of wax!" [71] More than ten years were to pass, apparently, before Tennyson found it in his hero's heart to utter the words of charity that appear in the published poem.[72]

The story of *Maud* is, in some measure, the same story, developed, deepened, and expanded, that we have seen before in "Locksley Hall" and "Edwin Morris": a young man, idealistic but morbid, passionate but poor, loves the beautiful girl in the mansion house, whose family oppose his suit and, as in "Edwin Morris," break angrily in upon their clandestine meeting in the family garden; a scene follows, and the hero departs the country. Here again is the wealthy suitor whose courtship is supported by the family for economic reasons and who is despised in extravagant terms by the hero:

49

> . . . a lord, a captain, a padded shape,
> A bought commission, a waxen face,
> A rabbit mouth that is ever agape—
> Bought? what is it he cannot buy?

And moving beneath the strange story is, in a much higher degree, the same intense and passionate sympathy of poet with dramatic spokesman.

The hero finds an appropriate (and for Tennyson familiar) symbol for his lyrical passion in the imagery of the rose which, as critics have often noted, is a major thematic strand in the poem.[73] A central example of this imagery is the passage where the hero waits for Maud in her garden, after the dance in the Hall and before his quarrel with Maud's brother:

> Queen rose of the rosebud garden of girls,
>   Come hither, the dances are done,
> In gloss of satin and glimmer of pearls,
>   Queen lily and rose in one;
> Shine out, little head, sunning over with curls,
>   To the flowers, and be their sun.
>
> There has fallen a splendid tear
>   From the passion-flower at the gate.
> She is coming, my dove, my dear;
>   She is coming, my life, my fate;
> The red rose cries, "She is near, she is near";
>   And the white rose weeps, "She is late";
> The larkspur listens, "I hear, I hear";
>   And the lily whispers, "I wait."
>
> She is coming, my own, my sweet;
>   Were it ever so airy a tread,
> My heart would hear her and beat,
>   Were it earth in an earthy bed;
> My dust would hear her and beat,
>   Had I lain for a century dead;

Would start and tremble under her feet,
  And blossom in purple and red.
"It was always delightful to [Rosa] to believe," says Rawnsley, "that the 'rose of the rosebud garden of girls,' had reference to her." Of all the rose passages in Tennyson, this was a strangely intense one for her to choose; and yet she—"Sole rose of beauty, loveliness complete," whose foot was "so light on field, or floor" —had indeed at least one memory of a passionate episode after a dance to make her think as she did; and in perusing the other lyrics in the poem she might have fancied that she caught an echo of verses she had heard before. Tennyson had written, we remember:

> Rose of roses, bliss of blisses,
> Rosebud-lips for honey-kisses;
> East and West and North and South
> Bear not such a rose as this is.

While the hero of *Maud* says:

> Rosy is the West,
> Rosy is the South,
> Roses are her cheeks,
> And a rose her mouth.

And Tennyson:

> The night with sudden odour reel'd,
> The southern stars a music peal'd,
> Warm beams across the meadow stole;
> For Love flew over grove and field,
> Said, "Open, Rosebud, open, yield
>   Thy fragrant soul."

And the hero of *Maud:*

> Come into the garden, Maud,
>   I am here at the gate alone;
> And the woodbine spices are wafted abroad,
>   And the musk of the rose is blown.
>
> For a breeze of morning moves,
>   And the planet of Love is on high.

Despite their knowledge that Tennyson abominated such identifications, Rawnsley and his brother Willingham were very fond of saying that the "high Hall-garden" of *Maud* had its original in the raised terrace garden of Harrington,[74] perhaps for no other reason than that they were struck by the likeness.[75] But the fact that today the garden of Harrington is called "Maud's garden" because of a tradition originated by the Rawnsleys, and a little room in the house (of which I will have more to say in a moment) called "Maud's room" for the same reason,[76] makes all the more interesting the report to me by one of the Rawnsleys of the present generation that she had always been given to believe that Rosa Baring was in some sense the original of the heroine of *Maud*.[77] Be that as it may, the resemblances between the Hall in *Maud* and Harrington Hall are, in view of Tennyson's attachment to Rosa, quite striking. Tennyson, as we know from "Roses on the Terrace," would, like the hero of *Maud*, have known his beloved's "own rose garden," and looking toward the garden from the meadows in front of Harrington, he would have seen "her pass like a light," "up in the high Hall-garden." And he would have heard, walking toward Harrington from Somersby, the rooks flying out from the rookery behind the garden "crying and calling" "Maud, Maud, Maud."[78] But more telling than these general correspondences are the details of the following passage:

> Maud's own little oak-room
> Which Maud, like a precious stone
> Set in the heart of the carven gloom,
> Lights with herself, . . .

Thinking of this passage dramatically, we remember that the hero, *persona non grata* in Maud's family, does not visit the house and has not seen the inside of it, if ever, since he "play'd with the girl when a child." He cannot very easily know which of the rooms in the Hall is Maud's, nor can he logically know what its interior is like. But Tennyson must have known quite well the small, very ornately and peculiarly carved oak-paneled room on the ground floor of Harrington, which in Victorian times would have made a fine sitting room for a young woman.[79]

However much Tennyson's memories of Rosa and her home may have entered into the poem, they by no means account for all of its content. Many other memories, edited, exaggerated, and combined, blended in the poem in many ways, so that, though Maud's father, like Arthur Eden, was "ever in London"[80] and the despised suitor was, like Shafto, rich from coal, they are not at all, I think, simple counters for Tennyson's feeling for these two men. But the complex sources of *Maud* must be left for study in the last chapter. Meanwhile it seems fair to say that the figure of Maud and the hero's ecstatic passion for her were built in part upon Tennyson's latent memories of Rosa and his strong associations of her with the flower for which she was named and the home, with its rose garden, in which she lived.[81]

It is therefore interesting to know that in June, 1854, after he had completed Part III of *Maud* but before he had written the earlier parts, Tennyson was directly reminded of Rosa probably for the first time in years. Sophy Rawnsley Elmhirst had apparently written him to say that the Shaftos were vacationing on the seacoast of the Isle of Wight, where Tennyson lived. Tennyson replied: "I did not know that Rosa was at Ryde. I hope that you will be coming to see her & if so that you will come on here."[82] It may mean something that Tennyson does not say he will either visit Rosa himself or invite her to Farringford, as he invites Sophy; but whatever his feelings in that regard, the knowledge that Rosa was only a few miles away from him might have stirred up memories which may still have been operating when, in September, 1854, as he was very busy writing the first two parts of *Maud*, he recited to F. T.

Palgrave the "Early Verses of Compliment to Miss Rosa Baring." [83]

Only one other poem invites brief consideration in this attempt to infer from Tennyson's writing the effect upon him of his early love. Turning over his Malory, Tennyson was apparently struck by the brief story of the hopeless, jealous love of the knight Pelleas for the beautiful but cold Ettard, "a great lady in her land"; of Pelleas' hopeless wanderings outside her castle, and of her unfaithfulness with Gawaine. [84] The story fitted very well, of course, into Tennyson's epic vision of a society destroyed by lust, and he told it with marked sympathy and understanding. Tennyson's Pelleas is naïve and idealistic, with little experience of women; for "out of the waste islands had he come, / Where saving his own sisters he had known / Scarce any but the women of his isles." And so he is overwhelmed by the sight of the beautiful Ettarre:

> "Is Guinevere herself so beautiful?"
> For large her violet eyes look'd, and her bloom
> A rosy dawn kindled in stainless heavens,
> And round her limbs, mature in womanhood;
> And slender was her hand and small her shape;
> And but for those large eyes, the haunts of scorn,
> She might have seem'd a toy to trifle with,
> And pass and care no more. But while he gazed
> The beauty of her flesh abash'd the boy,
> As tho' it were the beauty of her soul:
> For as the base man, judging of the good,
> Puts his own baseness in him by default
> Of will and nature, so did Pelleas lend
> All the young beauty of his own soul to hers.

Perhaps it is arbitrary to associate this passage with Rosa, and yet it is at least interesting that Ettarre shares her violet eyes with only two other of Tennyson's heroines—Maud, and Rose, the Gardener's Daughter —and that Rosa's own eyes were, to judge from her portrait, like Maud's, blue as violets. And it is at least interesting to compare Ettarre's round limbs and slender hand and small shape with Rosa's "full form and slender moulded waist." And it is interesting, too, to reflect that Tennyson's youthful realization that he had imputed to the beauty of a girl his own ideal spirit had led him to ask, "How thought you that this thing could captivate?" and to realize that "The form, the form alone is eloquent." But most interesting of all is the song which Pelleas muses on as he begins to suspect that Ettarre has betrayed him with Gawaine, a song with no place in the first edition but inserted as a unit later.[85]

> "A rose, but one, none other rose had I,
> A rose, one rose, and this was wondrous fair,
> One rose, a rose that gladden'd earth and
>   sky,
> One rose, my rose, that sweeten'd all mine
>   air—
> I cared not for the thorns; the thorns were
>   there.

> "One rose, a rose to gather by and by,
> One rose, a rose to gather and to wear,
> No rose but one—what other rose had I?
> One rose, my rose; a rose that will not die,—
> He dies who loves it,—if the worm be there."

This song "Pelleas had heard sung before the Queen." One wonders what jilted troubadour might have written it, and how long before.

That Tennyson, when he wrote these poems, associated them consciously or unconsciously with memories of Rosa seems to me indubitable; but I am unwilling, on the other hand, to draw from them any very firm conclusions as to what his relationship to her had actually been, since, whatever their emotional origin and associations, the poems are consciously artistic formulations incorporating considerable elements of conventional melodrama and imaginative exaggeration. But certain inferences, hedged round with doubts, may nonetheless legitimately be drawn. Tennyson must surely have been much more strongly attached to Rosa at one time than any student, except perhaps Sir Charles, has supposed; and surely he must have felt, with what justice we cannot know, that she had in some sense betrayed him. He must have felt as well some jealousy of Duncombe Shafto, and strong resentment of the part Rosa's parents played in bringing about the Rosa-Shafto marriage. I am even tempted to imagine that there may have been some slight biographical foundation for the unpleasant scenes in "Edwin Morris" and *Maud* in which the heroine's family interrupt the lovers' clandestine meeting. Such an assumption would at least help us to understand the bitterness which suffuses those scenes,[86] and it would explain the puzzling reference, noticed above, to the occasion when Amy "shrank, and put me from her" and the equally puzzling "trustees" of "Edwin Morris." But farther than this—and even probably so far—it is dangerous to go.

Whatever the nature of the "facts of lives real or imagined" which lay behind the poems, they themselves remain as enduring testimony to the impact those facts had upon Tennyson's psyche. It is genuinely remarkable how Tennyson's memory of his feeling for Rosa, and of the places and events with which that feeling was associated, persisted over his long life to find expression in such similar and yet different poetical ways.[87] The first of the poems, "Locksley Hall," was probably a nearly direct effect of feelings still very much in the foreground of his mind. The situation in the poem could have been nothing more than a subjective correlative of the situation from which his emotions sprang—enough like it that Tennyson could discharge through the speaker sentiments (probably secretly nourished and magnified) which he would otherwise not have been able to express at all; enough unlike it that he could escape conscious responsibility for whatever his overwrought speaker ("but I *know* my words are wild") chose to say. It was indeed his very ambiguous relation to the speaker which made "Locksley Hall" the paradoxical compound it is of melodramatic unreality and painfully intimate confession; Tennyson could not fully recognize, perhaps, and thus could not fully free himself from, the burden of jealous feeling which surged beneath the poem.

In the bittersweet idyl "Edwin Morris," begun a year or so later than "Locksley Hall," Tennyson was able to contemplate his memories of Rosa more objectively, and so, appropriately, he chose a spokesman who was also at some distance from his frustration and thus was able to take a less feverish view of it than the speaker of "Locksley Hall." Still, a good deal of bitterness remained, and more than a decade passed before Tennyson was able to set down the closing lines of psychic reconciliation with "Letty" in a passage which probably preserved the essential emotional truth of his own mellowing recollections of Rosa.

There, one would think, it might have ended, except that in 1854, as Tennyson turned back to the "O that 'twere possible" verses, he began to build around them a dramatic structure into which many resuscitated memories of his early life began to blend. With them came the memory of Rosa and the flower and hall with which, in Tennyson's imagination, she had become so deeply identified, to form what was still for him apparently a potent image of the physically beautiful— and sensually desirable—woman. But whereas Amy and Letty, I think, had been pretty much direct surrogates for Rosa, Maud was, as I have indicated, a much more complicated creation, deriving only par-

57

tially from Rosa and involving a much more liberated use of her memory.

In the 'sixties Tennyson found himself for some reason specially oppressed by a strong sense of man's sinful carnality, a near-obsession that found expression most obviously in "Lucretius" and the "Idylls of the King," [88] and this fact helps to explain the reappearance of the Rosa-figure, still recognizable beneath the garb of fantasy, in "Pelleas and Ettarre." Tennyson must have realized long before that his attraction to Rosa had been more a sensual infatuation than a rational love, and he must have come to recognize that, like Pelleas, he had been betrayed by "double-natured love" [89] into imputing to the physical form upon which his imagination had dwelt with such loving fascination a corresponding spiritual value which Rosa simply lacked. And something of the lingering guilt and shame which in darker moods he may retrospectively have felt may have found their way into the story of the icy-cold Ettarre and the young knight who came to realize that "I never loved her, I but lusted for her." [90]

But by the time of "Locksley Hall Sixty Years After," his memories of a dark past lightened by contrast with a still darker present, the old poet could remember Rosa tranquilly as the "slighter ghost" which, in comparison with Emily, she undoubtedly was, with little of the religious faith and spiritual radiance that enabled Emily to link for Tennyson "the broken chain that bound me to my kind." [91] And finally he was able, in the deep serenity he found before his death, to lay the mask aside and to remember Rosa intensely, tenderly, but with completely liberated aesthetic objectivity, in those lines which take on so much more beauty when one realizes what lay behind them:

Rose, on this terrace fifty years ago,
    When I was in my June, you in your May,
Two words, "*My* Rose," set all your face
        aglow,

> And now that I am white, and you are
> > gray,
> That blush of fifty years ago, my dear,
> > Blooms in the Past, but close to me to-day
> As this red rose, which on our terrace here
> > Glows in the blue of fifty miles away.

There the story might appropriately end, but one last ironic fact deserves to be recorded. Rosa, who must have been largely unaware of the stir she had made in the mind of the great poet, outlived him six years, long enough to read the *Memoir* published by his son. Blind and unable to write, she employed the clear hand of an amanuensis to set down her reaction: "Commenced reading Tennyson's Life," the diary says; and then, a day or so after, "Always reading the 'Life of Lord Tennyson'—Very delightful—The Life of a real Poet. Saw very few people on account of my cold." She died a few months after.

3

Sophy Rawnsley and Emily Sellwood

TENNYSON's early feeling for Sophy Rawnsley was probably less important than his attachment to Rosa Baring, but there are reasons nonetheless to think it significant. Sophy was the daughter of the Reverend Thomas Hardwicke Rawnsley, Rector of Halton Holgate, close friend of Tennyson's father, and the guardian after 1831 of his friend's children. Tennyson knew Sophy from her birth in 1818 [1] and watched her grow through all the stages of her girlhood into a gay and sprightly young woman. It was with thoughts of her, the Rawnsleys of a later generation always said, that he wrote "Airy, Fairy Lilian": [2]

> Airy, fairy Lilian,
> Flitting, fairy Lilian,
> When I ask her if she love me,
> Claps her tiny hands above me,
> Laughing all she can;
> She'll not tell me if she love me,
> Cruel little Lilian, . . .

Since, when this poem was published in 1830, Sophy was only twelve or thirteen, Tennyson twenty-one, the association would seem somewhat doubtful, except that the Rawnsleys have a strong supporting witness in

Emily Tennyson, Alfred's sister, who wrote in 1835 to Ellen Hallam:

> We had a party to dinner last Thursday, and finished the day with dancing, the evening was so very warm, that I do not know when I have felt so oppressed and fatigued as I did that night when all was over—there was a great deal of waltzing— a Miss Rawnsley who was here, is the lightest and most indefatigable dancer I ever saw,—she is a very nice amiable girl, and so cheerful and happy, that it brings sunshine into one's heart, though it were gloomy before, to look at her. Alfred is delighted with her. I sometimes fancy she is the prototype of his "Airy Fairy Lillian."[3]

H. D. Rawnsley tells most of what we know about Sophy and Tennyson in his *Memories,* where he discusses her together with Rosa Baring. He says in part:

> I often talked with my Aunt Sophy about Tennyson, and I found that the kind of awe with which he had inspired her had not passed away. "He was," she said, "so interesting because he was so unlike other young men, and his unconventionality of manner and dress had a charm which made him more acceptable than the dapper young gentleman of the ordinary type, at ball or supper party. He was a splendid dancer, for he loved music, and kept such time, but, you know," she would say, "we liked to talk better than to dance together, at Horncastle, or Spilsby, or Halton; he always had something worth saying, and said it so quaintly. Most girls were frightened of him. I was never afraid of the man, but of his mind."[4]

Aunt Sophy must have told Rawnsley a bit more than this, for, usually so cautious, he is bold enough to say: "That he was much attached to her in his days of calf-love cannot, I think, well be doubted." His attachment, whatever its character, did not come in his days of calf-love, for he could scarcely have regarded Sophy as a woman before he himself was at least twenty-five.

He was just that old when, in the year after Hallam's death, he wrote the first of two surviving poems to her:

> Sweet, ask me not why I am sad,
> But, when sad thoughts arise,
> Look on me, make my spirit glad
> To gaze upon thine eyes.
> For how can sorrow dwell in mine
> If they might always gaze on thine?

Though the lines have a tincture of rather wan romantic feeling, they do not go beyond the limits of conventional compliment. Two years later, it seems, she inspired a more significant poem:

TO SOPHY, 1836

> To thee, with whom my best affections
>   dwell,
> That I was harsh to thee, let no one know;
> It were, O Heaven! a stranger tale to tell
> Than if the vine had borne the bitter sloe:
> Tho' I was harsh, my nature is not so:
> A momentary cloud upon me fell:
> My coldness was mistimed like summer-
>   snow;
> Cold words I spoke, yet loved thee warm and
>   well.
> Was I so harsh? Ah, dear, it could not be.
> Seem'd I so cold? What madness moved my
>   blood
> To make me thus belie my constant heart
> That watch't with love thine earliest infancy,
> Slow-ripening to the grace of womanhood,
> Thro' every change that made thee what
>   thou art.[5]

This poem was sent to Sophy, Rawnsley says, after the same dance which was the occasion of Tennyson's intense lines of apology to Rosa Baring, so that he would seem to have fallen out at once with both girls, who were, we are told, "rivals for his society, perhaps for his admiration." But in the copies of these poems owned by Rawnsley's mother,[6] the one to Rosa is marked "Lines written by Alfred Tennyson after a quarrel at a Horncastle or a Spilsby Ball. 1836," while "To Sophy" (also dated 1836) is labeled "Sent to her after a little tiff at a Spilsby ball." Rawnsley's mother, who apparently wrote these comments, might have indicated more clearly than this the fact of their common origin, but in the absence of other information, we can scarcely doubt Rawnsley's story, which he may well have had from Rosa or Sophy herself.

Sophy's poem, not nearly so intense as Rosa's, is more direct, conversational, and assured. Tennyson talks of love, but it is clear from the context that he speaks in a generalized and not specially romantic sense. The poem is strongly and warmly affectionate rather than amorous. A letter Tennyson wrote to Sophy sometime in the 'thirties tells us more about his feeling but has pretty much the same tone as the poems:

> Dear Sophie,
>
> This is to let you know that you need not refrain from bestowing a tender osculation on whom-have-I-in-Heaven from fear of imparting any infection less tender than that of the heart, as Mr. Snaith pronounces the rubescence on the back of my hand to be nothing but a slight irregularity of the liver, which indeed the old Romans took to be the seat of love.
>
> May 18   I am, dear Sophie,
>   always yours
>   AT [7]

It would be going too far to read much into this gentle insinuation of romantic attachment, but there is nevertheless reason to think that at some time Tennyson's feeling grew genuinely serious. Sir Charles reports a tradition, in the village where Sophy's husband was rector, that Tennyson once proposed marriage to her.[8]

The tradition receives confirmation in a letter written by Sophy's grandson, who says: "I do know that Airy Fairy Lilian and her husband were on very good terms with Tennyson even though she had refused him half a dozen times and that he stayed with them for long periods at Shawell." [9] Such a tradition cannot be accorded the confidence given to a contemporary document or firsthand reminiscence, but the legend could hardly have grown without some basis in fact.

When, if ever, Tennyson might have proposed to Sophy can only be guessed, but it cannot have been before she was eighteen, that is to say, in or after 1836. By that year Tennyson's infatuation with Rosa Baring had probably subsided, and Sophy, now mature, might have been attractive to him. But, on the other hand, if we trust the evidence of the "Bridesmaid" sonnet, his feeling for Emily Sellwood was then already in progress. Yet we do not know how long before their quasi-engagement in 1838 Tennyson and Emily were exclusively committed to each other; during the earlier part of the years 1836–1838 Tennyson may have been free to do with his feelings what he would, perhaps to direct them toward Sophy. I am led to speculate in this way by one very uncertain but intriguing piece of evidence. In the *Memoir* Hallam Tennyson quotes "To thee with whom my best affections dwell" with the remark that Tennyson wrote it "at the end of 1837 or the beginning of 1838." [10] Hallam was very careless in dating his documents, but his statement here is curiously precise, as if he had in mind some definite span of time to which the verses belonged. There is no reason to suppose that his dating is any more correct than Rawnsley's, but the fact that he was willing to attribute this rather personal poem to a period just before his father's engagement suggests that he knew that there had been in 1837–1838 some attachment to Sophy on Tennyson's part. But whether there was or not, we shall probably never definitely know.

Whatever happened between Tennyson and Sophy in the 'thirties, they remained good friends after Tennyson's engagement in 1838 and Sophy's marriage in 1840 to the Reverend Edward Elmhirst;[11] and a few of Tennyson's letters to her have come down to give us the tone of their later relationship. Despite the fact that Tennyson was in the 'forties often with the Elmhirsts, only one of the surviving letters (quoted above) was written before Tennyson's marriage. Most of them (there are fourteen in all) date from the early 'fifties and are largely taken up with Tennyson's excuses for not visiting Sophy and his explanations and remonstrances when she imagines his refusals to be slights. All the letters are interesting, but two extracts will serve our present purposes:

... Now I feel hurt at the letter you have written me. You ought to have known me better than to have accused me of expressing myself as annoyed at your invitation. I was really amazed at your accusation & took some pains to inquire what you could mean. ... Sophy, Sophy, how could you? under whose influence are you acting to misinterpret so unhappily? I had really fancied that you did know a little more of me & that I am not the weathercock of change you would make me. Really your note is not kind & to sign yourself Yours &c &c makes it worse. I do not love unkind things to be thought said or done, & least of all did I expect it of *you*. ...

... pray do not suffer yourself to be so swayed again by tongues. Things in this foolish world of ours do get so distorted by heat & misapprehension & sometimes by downright lies that I have long made it a rule to believe in what I know not what I hear. I *know* my friends. I do not mean chance companions; & knowing them shall I

65

credit [two undecipherable words] & malicious hints of that wide-mouthed fool, society. No I will stick by them & bear them out till the end, whatever talk I hear. Gossip is my total abhorrence: I wish it were some living crawling thing that I might tread it out for ever. So again exhorting you dear Sophy to believe me because you have known me from your cradle & because you *know* me incapable of saying unkind things— & with Emily's love

I am yours affectionately
A Tennyson [12]

We conclude from these and the other records that throughout his life Tennyson had a warm, perhaps a special, feeling for Sophy, which may at some point have risen to courtship. But his attraction to her can never have been the troubled infatuation that he apparently felt for Rosa Baring. He speaks to Sophy always, in poems and letters alike, in a spirit of tenderness, trust, and unclouded affection. It is significant that in the Rawnsley account she and Rosa appear paired in his admiration. We guess from this and from other evidence that his attachments to them rose out of emotional needs which were to some extent mutually exclusive. To the one he was drawn passionately by richly feminine beauty and physical splendor; to the other by qualities of gaiety, vivacity, and probably common interest and good sense. We remember Sophy's remark that in the early days they liked better to talk than to dance. Perhaps it was because of Sophy's very different character that Tennyson may have turned for a time, during or after the frustration of his passion for Rosa, to a more rational if more mundane courtship of Rosa's friend. But, as we know, his attractions to both Rosa and Sophy failed to achieve permanence, possibly in part because Rosa lacked the spiritual resources of Sophy and Sophy the compelling emotional magnetism of Rosa. In Emily Sellwood, apparently, he found both the one quality and the other.

II

Though their families had been acquainted some years before,[13] Tennyson first met Emily, the *Memoir* tells us, in 1830:

> The Sellwoods had driven over one spring day from Horncastle, to call at Somersby Rectory. Arthur Hallam was then staying with the Tennysons; and asked Emily Sellwood to walk with him in the Fairy Wood. At a turn of the path they came upon my father, who, at sight of the slender, beautiful girl of seventeen in her simple gray dress, moving "like a light across those woodland ways," suddenly said to her: "Are you a Dryad or an Oread wandering here?" [14]

Despite the impression she seems to have made upon him then, the two saw little of each other, according to the *Memoir,* until the marriage of Tennyson's brother Charles, in May, 1836, to Emily's sister Louisa.[15] Meanwhile, as we have seen, Tennyson had become infatuated with the beautiful Rosa Baring and was drawn for a time also to Sophy Rawnsley. It is obvious, however, that Tennyson found Emily a much more satisfactory object of love than either of the other two girls had been. Rosa, Tennyson wrote in 1835 or 1836, was an icy jewel, frozen from chilly dews in which nature had "never dropt a human tear." He was drawn to Emily, in significant contrast, precisely because, when he saw her at Charles' wedding, she was able to feel and to weep:

> O Bridesmaid, ere the happy knot was tied,
> Thine eyes so wept that they could hardly
> see;
> Thy sister smiled and said, "No tears for me!
> A happy bridesmaid makes a happy bride."

And then, the couple standing side by side,
Love lighted down between them full of glee,
And over his left shoulder laugh'd at thee,
"O happy bridesmaid, make a happy bride."
And all at once a pleasant truth I learn'd,
For while the tender service made thee weep,
I loved thee for the tear thou couldst not hide,
And prest thy hand, and knew the press
    return'd,
And thought, "My life is sick of single sleep;
O happy bridesmaid, make a happy bride!"

This declaration of tender love is clear enough, and it
may well be that from 1836 onward Tennyson was
emotionally committed to Emily. But the *Memoir* says
only that they became "quasi-engaged" in 1838,[16] so
that developments in the interval are uncertain.

After the troubles of 1835–1837 and the removal
from Somersby, Tennyson must have been at nearly the
low point of his spiritual development; we may gauge
the over-all effect of those years from his description
of himself to Milnes (in January, 1837) as a "nervous,
morbidly-irritable man, down in the world, stark-
spoiled with the staggers of a mismanaged imagination
and quite opprest by fortune and the reviews." [17] The
self-estimate was too true to be very funny. But in 1838,
after the removal from Somersby, came the correspondence and semi-engagement to Emily, and for the first
time in four years his spirits seem to have appreciably
lightened. The engagement, writes Hallam Tennyson,
"again braced my father for the struggle of life. The
current of his mind no longer ran constantly in the
channel of mournful memories and melancholy fore-
bodings." Tennyson was "on the whole happy in his
life, and looked forward to still better days." [18] He was
very quickly at work again, and he wrote in the years
of the correspondence many of the new poems which,
together with those already published in 1833 and the
cluster written in the months after Hallam's death,

were to make up the 1842 volumes.[19] Emily was a very powerful cordial.

Although most of the 1838–1840 correspondence was burned, at Tennyson's direction, the fragments which have survived [20] tell us that he found in Emily, more than anything else, understanding and spiritual comfort. Tennyson had always had a conception of the pure woman as a redeemer of troubled man, and the idea had been given definite shape in his mind by Hallam's neo-Dantean philosophy. "A good woman," Tennyson wrote to Emily, "is a wondrous creature, cleaving to the right and good in all change; lovely in her youthful comeliness, lovely all her life long in comeliness of heart." [21] Emily herself was such a woman. More than Rosa Baring or Sophy Rawnsley could ever have been, Emily was a woman kindred of his soul. Although she was very attractive, with her "tender, spiritual face," Tennyson was drawn to her, not by physical beauty as he had been to Rosa, but primarily by qualities of mind and heart. She is a "white dove, brooding in thy lonely chamber"; he feels deeply her "superiority in all that is good"; she is "so much stronger and holier" than he; he needs her "assurances to make up the deficiencies in my own strength." "If thy love for me is a strengthening influence to thyself, so shall mine for thee be to myself." [22] His affection for her, as for Hallam, was an ennobling affection, her spiritual radiance a guide light to his own idealistic but troubled spirit.

But Alfred was to have the comfort of communication with Emily only till 1840. After that date, says Hallam Tennyson, the correspondence was forbidden.[23] Hallam's statement has usually been understood to mean that the responsibility for the breaking off of the relationship lay with Mr. Sellwood, but, as a matter of fact, the decision to part seems to have been in large measure Alfred's and Emily's. The fullest account of the matter is printed in Hallam Tennyson's *Materials for a Life of A.T.*; the writer is a Mr. Symington, who had his facts from Alfred's brother, Charles Tennyson Turner:

> After telling me that your father had been engaged to his sister-in-law, (for some years after 1837), he said that Alfred found that his monetary position did not improve as he expected, and he got into low and desponding spirits as to his future prospects; and from a sense of honour, though sorely against the grain, came to think that under the circumstances it was unjust and unfair in him to hold your mother bound. His own mother had such a high opinion of his choice that she offered to share her jointure with him to enable him to marry. This, however, Alfred Tennyson and Emily Sellwood refused as being unjust to his brothers and sisters. So the engagement was broken off. Mr. Turner added that the love between your father and mother continued unshaken, and that but for an overstrained, morbid scrupulousness as to what was conceived to be duty, they might have been contented to wait (an engaged couple), and so both might have been spared much suffering.[24]

This account is confirmed by a careful reading of a passage in a letter Tennyson wrote to Emily in December, 1839, fragments of which have been printed by Sir Charles in his biography. The letter was written, one notices, some months before the correspondence was forbidden:

> How should this dependence on thy state co-exist with my flying from thee? ask not. Believe that it does. Tis true, I fly for my good, perhaps for thine, at any rate for thine if mine is thine. If thou knewest why I fly thee there is nothing thou would'st more wish for than that I should fly thee. Sayest thou "are we to meet no more?" I answer I know not the word nor will know it. I neither know it nor believe it. The immortality of man

disdains and rejects it—the immortality of man to which the cycles and the Aeons are as hours and as days.[25]

Exactly what Tennyson is saying here is not completely clear, but he plainly communicates his decision not to see Emily any more, for reasons which she does not wholly understand. But though he thus cut himself off from direct contact with her and made no commitment as to their future, his action apparently did not mean that he would not continue to write to her, for the correspondence kept on till June or July, 1840.[26] Considering the fact that Tennyson himself thus refused engagement, it is no wonder that Henry Sellwood should have intervened. It seems a clear inference, both from Symington's account and from Tennyson's letter, that what Sellwood finally forbade was not an engagement but only a correspondence which Alfred had himself decided could not then lead to a formal arrangement.

"Love and Duty," a poem about the separation which appears to be almost literally autobiographical, puts emphasis solely on the decision of the lover(s), with no allusion to any external authority:

> For Love himself took part against himself
> To warn us off, and Duty loved of Love—
> O this world's curse,—beloved but hated—
>   came
> Like Death betwixt thy dear embrace and
>   mine,
> And crying, " Who is this? behold thy bride,"
> She push'd me from thee.
>   If the sense is hard
> To alien ears, I did not speak to these—
> No, not to thee, but to thyself in me.
> Hard is my doom and thine; thou knowest it
>   all.

The meaning, here and elsewhere in the poem, is hard indeed; but the reason for the separation is manifestly clear: Tennyson's and Emily's sense of duty; more particularly, Alfred's sense of duty, since he speaks here and in the letter "not to thee, but to thyself in me." [27]

That sense of duty was, says Symington, an "overstrained, morbid scrupulousness." What lay behind it? First of all, of course, Tennyson's lack of funds, "the eternal want of pence," mentioned by Hallam Tennyson.[28] Alfred had only a small inheritance of £3000 or so, the income from which could scarcely support a respectable marriage, especially since he was obdurately opposed to any vocation except poetry. But Tennyson's economic situation only explains why they did not marry; it does not explain, as Symington's remarks indicate, why they did not remain engaged until some future time when marriage might become possible. The real explanation, I think, is that Tennyson chose to leave Emily because her family was opposed to him, because this fact caused pain to Emily, and because he himself was not sure that he was worthy of her plighted love.

The family would have been uncomfortable about the relationship, first of all, because Charles's marriage to Louisa had been a tragic failure, as Charles had plunged once more into his old narcotic addiction and his wife's health broke under the consequent strain.[29] The Sellwoods would not have been anxious for another such alliance, even had Alfred been less poor than he was. Secondly, the strongly religious family had doubts of Alfred's orthodoxy, as is suggested by a passage from one of the fragments of his correspondence:

> If I have written aught of this from vanity may thy love leave me when I want it most. I scarce expect thee to agree with me in many things I have said—believe only that all is kindness to thee, to her, to Anne, to thy father and that I have but one wish with respect to them all, that they may be blest by the Father of all and that they may see the truth, not as I see it, (if not the truth) but the truth.[30]

The "her" referred to was, I think, Emily's Aunt Betsy, probably one of those "crones in or about Horncastle" whom Tennyson referred to a few years later as having been always "causelessly bitter against me and mine." [31] That the resultant situation was disquieting to Emily is implied in two sentences of the December, 1839, letter before the passage in which Tennyson seems to take leave of her: "Would to Heaven thou could'st be comfortable, that I might know thou wert in a restful state, not bowed beneath the burthen of the days. Ah that is a painful thing not to find sympathy by our own fireside, but if it cannot be, *if* God has varied his creature man in a million ways, what help but in ourselves?" [32]

Tennyson, knowing of the Sellwood family's opposition and painfully conscious that his life so far could not prove them wrong, must have felt that it would be unjust to ask Emily to commit herself to him while in his own view he had not yet proved himself worthy of that commitment and could not be sure that he ever would do so. His words in the letter, "I fly for my good, perhaps for thine, at any rate for thine if mine is thine. If thou knewest why I fly thee there is nothing thou would'st more wish for than that I should fly thee," were prompted, I think, by Tennyson's conviction that he must work out apart from Emily, for his sake and ultimately for hers, the spiritual integrity and peace, as well as the economic security and poetical success, which would permit him, fully justified in his eyes and the eyes of the world, to claim her for his bride. He could not, honorably and with a good conscience, allow the attachment to continue while he was still in process of becoming worthy of it.[33] "Wait," he says in "Love and Duty"; "my faith is large in Time, / And that which shapes it to some perfect end. . . . My work shall answer, since I knew the right / And did it." Firm in his conviction of his love for her, he looked toward a future created out of the fact of love which would justify him and the course of action he had taken and would permit him, eventually, to return to Emily. The last, of course, he could not say to her, for to say it would bind her when he had chosen not to bind her. He could only say:

> My blessing! Should my Shadow cross thy thoughts
> Too sadly for their peace, remand it thou
> For calmer hours to Memory's darkest hold,
> If not to be forgotten—not at once—
> Not all forgotten. Should it cross thy dreams,
> O might it come like one that looks content,
> With quiet eyes unfaithful to the truth,
> And point thee forward to a distant light,
> Or seem to lift a burthen from thy heart
> And leave thee freer, till thou wake refresh'd . . .

The couple seem, after the forbidding of the correspondence, to have had one last meeting ("Could Love part thus? was it not well to speak, / To have spoken once?"), for, although the opening section of "Love and Duty" seems to refer to the stage of the relationship manifested in the December letter, of which it is almost a paraphrase, the latter part memorializes a subsequent "summer" meeting which must have taken place in June or July, 1840, and during which they "bade adieu for ever."

In "Love and Duty" Tennyson pictures and rejects a possible sequel to his severed love which, in life, was more difficult to avoid. Shall the love, Tennyson asks,

> this wonder, dead, become
> Mere highway dust? or year by year alone
> Sit brooding in the ruins of a life,
> Nightmare of youth, the spectre of himself?
> If this were thus, if this, indeed, were all,
> Better the narrow brain, the stony heart,
> The staring eye glazed o'er with sapless days,
> The long mechanic pacings to and fro,
> The set gray life, and apathetic end.

74

Better, that is, the condition of the insane whom he recently had seen in Dr. Allen's establishment in High Beech, than the depressed, morbid broodings to which he knew himself to be subject. But, already, shortly after he wrote his letter in December, he had become, in FitzGerald's words, "really ill, in a nervous way," [34] a foreshadowing of more psychological malaise to come. But, recovering himself after the separation, he appears to have moved for a time in something of the tentatively confident spirit of "Love and Duty." He ventured on two positive steps: he decided, after hesitation, to publish again; and he plunged into Dr. Allen's scheme to capitalize on a process of mechanical wood carving. Hallam Tennyson specifically associates Tennyson's decision to publish with his need to "earn a livelihood on which to marry," [35] so that both actions were probably directly related to his desire to prove himself an effective social agent and to make him financially able to marry Emily, with whom he was still occasionally in indirect contact.[36] The 1842 volumes established his eminence as a poet, but did not bring in much money; the wood-carving project, into which he put so much enthusiasm, was a disastrous failure in which he lost his whole patrimony, plus an additional legacy of £500 left him by an aunt of Arthur Hallam's.[37] After this devastating blow, Hallam Tennyson writes, "so severe a hypochondria set in upon him that his friends despaired of his life. 'I have,' he writes, 'drunk one of those most bitter draughts out of the cup of life, which go near to make men hate the world they move in.'" [38]

The Allen project failed finally in early 1843; [39] by the end of the year Tennyson was undergoing the rigorous discipline of the water cure. FitzGerald, who had seen him just before, reported that he "looked, and said he was, ill: I have never seen him so hopeless . . . He would scarcely see any of us and went away suddenly." [40] This was in December; in February Alfred wrote Fitz to say:

It is very kind of you to think of such a poor body as myself—The perpetual panic and horror of the last two years had steeped my nerves in poison: now I am left a beggar, but I am or shall be shortly somewhat better off in nerves . . . They were so bad six weeks ago that I could not have written this, and to have to write a letter on that accursed business threw me into a kind of convulsion. I went through Hell. Thank you for inquiring after me. I am such a poor devil now I am afraid I shall very rarely see you. No more trips to London and living in London, hard penury and battle will be my lot.[41]

Tennyson's friends, especially FitzGerald, always suspected that there was a touch of willfullness and self-pity in Tennyson's illnesses, and undoubtedly there was. But the threat of real mental illness was always there. We cannot forget that the memory of his unbalanced father always hung over him and that four of his brothers had experienced serious emotional disturbances, one of them going literally insane.[42] Whatever of falsity there was in Tennyson's moods, there was also a definite element of genuine mental disorder with the possibility of serious derangement. Still, there was always deep within him a powerful sense of the strength of his genius and a confident intuition of his destiny. "Arthur," he had said to his brother in his youth, "I mean to be famous."[43] The Tennyson who said that was the Tennyson who, however dark his mental atmosphere grew, had always some glimpse of the Gleam.

But for some time after 1843 any hope of reunion with Emily must have been extinguished, even when in January, 1845, Dr. Allen died and, his life having been insured by the generous Edmund Lushington, Tennyson gained back the greater part of his lost inheritance.[44] In April, 1845, he told de Vere that he was "dreadfully cut up by all he had gone through," and in

July de Vere recorded a conversation in which Tennyson "railed against the whole system of society, and said he was miserable." What his mind was brooding on appears from de Vere's diary entry two days later:

> Tennyson . . . seemed much out of spirits, and said that he could no longer bear to be knocked about the world, and that he must marry and find love and peace or die. . . . He complained much about growing old, and said he cared nothing for fame, and that his life was all thrown away for want of a competence and retirement. Said that no one had been so much harassed by anxiety and trouble as himself. I told him he wanted occupation, a wife, and orthodox principles, which he took well.[45]

Later in the same year he told Lady Harriet Baring that he " 'must have a woman to live beside; would *prefer a lady,* but—cannot afford one; and so must marry a maid-servant.' "[46] Just after this he received, through the influence of Carlyle, Milnes, and others, a pension from Peel's government of £200 a year.[47] It was in a letter to T. H. Rawnsley telling of the pension that Tennyson shortly afterward made the reference quoted above to the "crones in or about Horncastle." "I wish them no worse punishment," he said, "than that they should read the very flattering letter Peel wrote me."

With the recovered money from the wood-carving and the pension he was certainly in some position to make a marriage offer, but he apparently made no move to do so. Why? Because, I think, his "work" had not yet fully "answered." He had been steadily at work, probably since late 1844, on *The Princess,* a poem which he had planned with Emily Sellwood in 1839.[48] Here he was to give his most copious statement of his fervent and idealistic views of the relationship of man and woman. I quote two passages which, Hallam Tennyson indicates, express convictions that the poet felt very strongly:

> Let this proud watchword rest
> Of equal; seeing either sex alone
> Is half itself, and in true marriage lies
> Nor equal, nor unequal: each fulfils
> Defect in each, and always thought in thought,
> Purpose in purpose, will in will, they grow,
> The single pure and perfect animal,
> The two-cell'd heart beating, with one full
>   stroke,
> Life.

> To love one maiden only, cleave to her,
> And worship her by years of noble deeds,
> Until they win her; for indeed I know
> Of no more subtle master under heaven
> Than is the maiden passion for a maid,
> Not only to keep down the base in man,
> But teach high thought and amiable words,
> And courtliness and the desire of fame,
> And love of truth, and all that makes a man.[49]

The poem was published in 1847 with considerable success and must have added a good bit to his income.[50] Now, after years of consecrated work, with the testament of his faith complete, with some income, the prospect of more, and a secure position as a poet, the time had come to speak. In late 1847 or 1848, accordingly, he approached Emily once more, proposed—and was rejected. The episode is not recorded in either of the standard biographies, but H. D. Rawnsley writes that seven years after the correspondence was cut off, "Tennyson again came forward and this time was refused on the highest and noblest principles of self-abnegation by the woman who had loved him." [51] There is no reason to doubt this definite statement made by a man whose mother (Catherine Rawnsley) was Emily's cousin and intimate, even had his brother not confirmed it in another place, saying that "Emily, in a letter to my mother, says that she had even definitely refused him [in 1848]." [52] What were Emily's reasons? She had grown to feel, says H. D. Rawnsley, "that they too moved in worlds of religious thought so different that the two would not 'make one music' as they moved." In 1840 Emily had probably shared to some extent the doubts felt by her family, a fact which may have contributed to Alfred's decision not to bind her in an engagement. Over the years, perhaps, these doubts had grown, aggravated possibly by rumors of Tennyson's unhealthy habits and the disorderly life which, despite his great poetic achievement, he had been leading.

We may gauge Tennyson's reaction to Emily's refusal by the fact that late in 1848 he was back again taking the water treatment, from which FitzGerald reported him emerging "half-cured, or half-destroyed"; "he now drinks a bottle of wine a day, and smokes as before; a sure way to throw back in a week or two all the benefit (if benefit there were) which resulted from many weeks of privation and penance." [53] Still, as de Vere writes, Alfred was "all in favour of marriage, and indeed will not be right till he has some one to love him exclusively." [54]

Within a year and a half negotiations for marriage were afoot once more, but how the union was finally arranged is not completely clear. Symington gives the most detailed account in the *Materials for a Life of A.T.*:

> Moxon [Tennyson's publisher], when on a visit to Alfred [in late 1849?], asked if he had been writing anything of late, with a view to publication. On which Alfred said emphatically, "No." Moxon then said, "Surely you have not been idle?" Alfred said that he had been writing, for his own relief and private satisfaction, some things that the public would have no interest in, and would not care to see. Moxon asked for the MS. It was "In Memoriam." Moxon was delighted and, to

Alfred's utter astonishment, offered to publish it, and to hand him a cheque on the spot, promising more. If my memory serves me, I think the amount was £300. On finding this unexpected opening, Alfred went to Charles, explained the situation, and thought the engagement might now be renewed, asking Charles to arrange a meeting for that purpose. Alfred assured him that the long separation had been on their (Alfred and Emily Sellwood's) parts a sacrifice and self-renunciation, and that he could not live without her, and *now,* that a way was opened up, all would come right. Charles was satisfied, and he added to me that *all along* he believed that they were mutually made for each other. He always regarded your father's and mother's union as a perfectly ideal marriage.[55]

Much of this must be doubted. The £300 advance can scarcely have been the reason of Alfred's coming forward again, since it cannot have made a really significant change in his already satisfactory circumstances; but on the other hand if he had made up his mind to try once more for a reconciliation, the money was a lump sum which would have made it easy to set up an establishment. Sir Charles Tennyson points out that some communication between the pair had been renewed by November 24, 1849, on which date Tennyson seems to have sent Emily a copy of "Sweet and Low" from *The Princess;* and he places Alfred's conversation with Charles in the first half of December, 1849,[56] so that Tennyson's solicitation of Charles would have followed rather than preceded a renewal of contact with Emily.

About the same time that he was seeing Charles, Alfred arranged to pay a visit to Drummond and Catherine Rawnsley at Shiplake,[57] and after the visit the Rawnsleys played a major role in furthering the reunion. "My mother," says W. F. Rawnsley, "obtained leave to send [a copy of *In Memoriam*] to Emily Sellwood, who wrote an excellent letter of heartfelt praise of 'The Elegies' . . . But she was almost afraid to send it." [58] The letter, dated April 1, 1850, suggests, as Sir Charles says, that "she was still far from a definite understanding with him": [59]

> . . . Do you really think I should write a line with the Elegies, that is in a separate note, to say I have returned them? I am almost afraid, but since you say I am to do so I will, only I cannot say what I feel . . . You and Drummond are among the best and kindest friends I have in the world, and let me not be ungrateful, I have some very good and kind. The longer I live the more I feel how blessed I am in this way. Now I must say goodbye—

> Thy loving sister, [60]
> Emily

> P.S. I thought I would write my note before the others came. Here it is, no beginning nor end, not a note at all, a sort of label only. "Katie told me the poems might be kept until Saturday. I hope I shall not have occasioned any inconvenience by keeping them to the limit of time; and if I have I must be forgiven, for I cannot willingly part from what is so precious. The thanks I would say for them and for the faith in me which has trusted them to me must be thought for me, I cannot write them. I have read the poems through and through and through and to me they were and they are ever more and more a spirit monument grand and beautiful, in whose presence I feel admiration and delight, not unmixed with awe. The happiest possible end to this labour of love! But think not its fruits shall so soon perish, for they are life in life, and they shall live, and as years go on be only the more fully known and loved and reverenced for what they are.

81

"So says a true seer. Can anyone guess the name of this seer? After such big words shall I put anything about my own little I?—that I am the happier for having seen these poems and that I hope I shall be the better too."

I cannot enter into things more particularly with him. I only hope he will not be vexed by this apology of a note.[61]

Emily felt unable, obviously, to address Alfred directly. Her diffidence arose, no doubt, from her earlier refusal of him, the circumstances of which she had probably explained to Mrs. Rawnsley in the missing part of this letter (see nn. 52 and 61).

Sir Charles is undoubtedly right in thinking that *In Memoriam* finally removed Emily's doubts as to Alfred's religion and cleared the way for the marriage.[62] Very soon after this letter, under the urgings of Catherine Rawnsley and Charles Kingsley, plans were under way for the wedding.

But at the end, strangely enough, it was Alfred who had doubts about the proceedings. This is evident from a lecture of W. F. Rawnsley's, which, though it offers the fullest available account of the marriage, has been oddly ignored by students of Tennyson. I quote at length:

On looking at the marriage license you would see that it is dated *May fifteenth,* though the wedding day was June 13th. The reason of this is, that my mother, who had undertaken to have the wedding from our house at Shiplake . . . found it impossible to get him to fix a date and stick to it. He was just then suffering from one of his fits of depression, which he once told me would come over him suddenly sometimes in a ball-room and which he only quite late in life discovered to be due to gout. The consequence was that he could not make up his mind, and he wrote to his mother only just before the wedding that he "should have written to let her know earlier, but that he did not know himself till just at last, as he could not make up his mind." His sister Mary also wrote in June, "Alfred maintains a cruel silence about his engagement, which I think is not fair towards his family, especially as the Rawnsleys know it."

The result of this depression was that the date of the wedding hung uncertain for some weeks, until owing, says his sister Mary, to the persuasion of Edmund and Cecilia Lushington, but really still more to my mother's insistence, he brought himself to name the day, and in the beginning of the month wrote to my mother:

Dear Kate,
    It is settled for the 13th, so the shirts may be gone on with.

His sister Mary, who had written in commiseration, "poor thing, I dare say he is miserable enough at times, thinking of what he is about to do," wrote afterwards of the wedding just as if it had been a funeral, beginning her letter: "Well, all is over. Alfred was married to Emily Sellwood last Friday. . . . . *Friday, and raining,* about which I feel very superstitious . . . . . . Emily looked bright, they say. They were married at the Drummond Rawnsleys and the Lushingtons were there. . . . We received this morning a beautiful piece of bridecake. I hope they will be happy, but I feel very doubtful about it." [63]

Mary Tennyson's letter is surprisingly grim. Perhaps she and the rest of the family were not happy about the finicky attitude the Sellwoods had taken toward Alfred; perhaps there were still open wounds from the troubles of Charles and Louisa. Mary's remarks certainly suggest that the arrangements for the wedding took place under something of a cloud. Alfred, we see, did not inform his family of his intentions; and Emily, for her part, neglected to inform her father fully of all the factors involved in her decision to marry, for she writes after the wedding to Kate Rawnsley, "Please tell my Daddy all except the In Memoriam." [64] More evidence that there was trouble at the time of the marriage is a letter Tennyson wrote on May 7, 1850, to his cousin Lewis Ffytche: "Pray dearest Lewis forgive me. I throw myself on your mercy. I took I know not what absurd fancies into my head & I have had enough perplexity & vexation this week to drive most men crazy. I have this moment only got your letter & beseech you to pardon me." [65]

"Perplexity & vexation" suggest largely external obstacles, probably from Emily's family, but some of Mary Tennyson's remarks imply that there were internal ones as well. Tennyson's doubts about the marriage, though scarcely the result of gout, may have had no deeper cause than the uncertainty produced in his complicated nature by the irrevocable step he was about to take. He had after all lived apart from Emily for many years, and he had probably had little opportunity at the Rawnsleys to become fully reacquainted with her. Perhaps this uncertainty was increased by lingering reluctance on Emily's part. If indeed he had doubts of her, he probably had much stronger doubts of himself and his own worthiness; that, at least, is the implication of a stanza of the verses in which, later, he celebrated the marriage:

> Good she is and pure and just.
> Being conquered by her sweetness,
> I shall come through her, I trust,
> Into fuller-orbed completeness,
> Though but made of erring dust.[66]

But with the wedding itself all doubts were dissolved. As Tennyson said in after years, "The peace of God came into my life before the altar when I married her." [67] After nearly two decades of despondency, of morbid brooding and spiritual alienation from society, he found in Emily a comfort such as he had never known. The long period of trouble which had extended, with occasional relief, from the time of Hallam's death, was over; and, as if to symbolize that fact, he took Emily immediately after the marriage to visit Hallam's tomb, which he had not seen before. " 'It seemed a kind of consecration to go there.' " [68]

There is ample testimony to the effect of the marriage on Tennyson. "I have never before had half so much pleasure in Alfred's society," wrote Aubrey de Vere in October; "he is far happier than I ever saw him before; and his 'wrath against the world' is proportionately mitigated. He has an unbounded respect for his wife, as well as a strong affection, which has been growing stronger ever since his marriage." [69] Patmore was equally impressed by the couple's happiness, and wrote of Emily: "She is highly cultivated, but her mind seems always deeper than her cultivation, and her heart always deeper than her mind. . . . Her religion is at once deep and wide"; "she has instruction and intellect enough to make the stock-in-trade of half-a-dozen literary ladies; but she is neither brilliant nor literary at all. Tennyson has made no hasty or ill-judged choice. She seems to understand him thoroughly, and, without the least ostentation or officiousness of affection, waits upon and attends to him as she ought to." [70]

But complete peace was yet at a distance. In the next three years there was the publicity of the Laureateship, the death of the first child, the constant movings about in search of a dwelling both sufficiently private and otherwise suitable for their needs, to keep the Tennysons from a secure sense of establishment in the world.[71] Finally, in the fall of 1853, they found in Farringford the home they had long sought. But even after some months there, in the spring of 1854, things were not entirely right. "We have hardly seen a human face since we came here," Tennyson wrote Patmore, "except the

85

members of our household. Happy, I certainly have not been. I entirely disagree with the saying you quote of happy men not writing poetry. Vexations (particularly long vexations of a petty kind) are much more destructive of the 'gay science,' as the Troubadours (I believe) called it." [72]

But it was just at this time, during the psychic crisis produced by the birth of Lionel and Emily's consequent illness, that he wrote the conclusion to *Maud*, with its significant lines:

> I have felt with my native land, I am one
> with my kind,
> I embrace the purpose of God, and the doom
> assign'd.

Later that year, as the countryside around him grew luxuriant in the warm long days of the Isle of Wight summer, his life took on a decided aspect of solid comfort and peace, reinforced by his new friendship with Sir John Simeon. It was then that he was able to compose the rest of *Maud*—an act of major autobiographical import which will be discussed in the last chapter of this book.

As *Maud* was in process of completion, de Vere came to visit the Tennysons and gave what we may take as a final judgment on a union now fully established:

> Certainly A. Tennyson has been very greatly blessed in his marriage; and he deserved it; for he seems to have been guided by the highest of motives, and to have followed the true wisdom of the heart, in his choice. He is much happier and proportionately less morbid than he used to be; and in all respects improved.

De Vere's estimate of Emily discloses the source of Alfred's happiness:

> I can hardly say how deeply interesting she is to me. She is a woman full of soul as well as mind, and in all her affections, it seems to me that it is in the soul, and for the soul, that she loves those

dear to her. She would, I have no doubt, make any imaginable sacrifice of her happiness to promote the real and interior good of her husband, and not of her happiness only, but of his also. . . . I regard her as one of the "few noble" whom it has been my lot to meet in life; and with a nature so generous, and so religious a use of the high qualities God has given her, I cannot but hope that the happiness accorded to her after so many years of trial, may be more and more blessed to her as the days go by.[73]

4

Maud *as Autobiography*

WE HAVE seen, in chapters i and iii something of the circumstances in which *Maud* was written—how it came during the settling in at Farringford which marked the end of the nomadic first years of Tennyson's marriage, which had itself marked the end of a long period of trouble extending back to the death of Hallam; and how he built the poem around "O that 'twere possible," a lyric written at the beginning of that period, in fulfillment of an intention which had probably been in his mind for some time. The lyric roused in him, apparently, many painful memories of the years which had passed since it was written, memories with which it was, as we shall see, in many intimate ways connected; for moving outward from the lyric, in what seems to have been a peculiarly piecemeal and patchwork fashion,[1] his imagination shaped in the curious mosaic of the whole monodrama a pattern which was an analogue of the pattern of his private life in those same years; so that the act of creation was also an act of cathartic recapitulation by which he defined and judged his early life and attempted to put it behind him. But in seeking to understand the poem as an autobiographical expression, we must begin not immediately with the events of 1834 and after, which because of their obscurity have so far been our concern, but with still earlier and better known circumstances in

Tennyson's life—also directly reflected in the poem—out of which in part the later events grew and in terms of which they must be understood.

I

Tennyson's youth was dominated by his father, Dr. George Clayton Tennyson, an intelligent, learned, and in many ways admirable man who nevertheless suffered from a congenitally dark temperament which, aggravated by external circumstances and an increasing inclination to drink, grew more unstable as the years went by, showing itself in ever more serious fits of despair, rage, and violence that left him incapacitated for his clerical duties and led finally to his premature death in 1831 at the age of fifty-three.[2] Though Tennyson was strongly attached to his father, the older man's erratic conduct, with its by-products of gossip and scandal, inevitably had a most unfortunate effect upon his hypersensitive son, generating inner tensions and feelings of guilt which left him painfully and permanently self-conscious and subject to brooding moods of depression and despair. His early anxieties were only intensified by his devotion to his mother, a saintly woman of strong Evangelical persuasions, whose life was rendered miserable before her husband's death by his terrifying instability and after it by legal and monetary difficulties which the frugality of her father-in-law, who controlled her family's finances, made more troublesome than they needed to be.

This basic situation has an obvious analogue in *Maud*. The hero is the "heir of madness," his whole life blighted by the influence of his "dark" father who, like Tennyson's, was wont to "rage in his mood"—"ah God, as he used to rave." The hero's father has died in ambiguous circumstances which strongly suggest suicide, whereas Tennyson's, of course, died a natural death;[3] but the poetic death is only a melodramatic exaggeration of the essential truth about the real one: Tennyson's father

89

did by his alcoholism in a very real sense destroy himself; he, too, had made "false haste to the grave." In
both poem and life it is the memory of the father's
erratic life, ending in a death tinged by scandal, which
is in large measure responsible for the son's alienation.
Pondering upon the tragic memory of his father and on
his lonely mother "so gentle and good," who is "vext
with lawyers and harass'd with debt," [4] the hero comes
like Tennyson to be gripped by a "morbid hate and
horror" of "a world in which I have hardly mixt." [5]

Tennyson's attitude toward his father was complicated by the fact that Dr. Tennyson had been very
badly used by his own father (George Tennyson, Sr.),
who had arbitrarily disinherited his eldest son in favor
of a younger one.[6] Charles Tennyson (later d'Eyncourt)
went on, with his father's wealth, to a successful career
in Parliament and lived in circumstances so comfortable
as to form a painful contrast with the hectic life at
Somersby Rectory, where the parents, eleven children,
and servants all lived together in a few rooms. Since
Alfred and the family certainly felt the injustice of the
disinheritance as strongly as the father himself, the
grandfather and uncle must always have seemed to
them the real cause of Dr. Tennyson's and thus of their
own multiplying troubles. In *Maud* it is not a grandfather but another "old man, now lord of the broad
estate and the Hall," who is the source of the family's
distresses. Through some financial skulduggery left very
vague in the poem, he and his son have "dropt off
gorged from a scheme that had left us flaccid and
drain'd." It is difficult not to see in this "gray old wolf"
—"the wrinkled head of the race"—Tennyson's grandfather, the "old man of the wolds," as the Somersby
children called him, and in his shadowy "scheme" the
disinheritance which deprived the father and (after his
death) the family of the social and economic status
which they felt was rightfully theirs. Closely identified
with the old man in the poem, and deeply involved in

"the feud / . . . By which our houses are torn," is his darkly handsome politician son, hated by the hero as the corresponding figure in Tennyson's own life, Charles Tennyson d'Eyncourt, was hated by him.[7]

Maud's family is intimately associated with another very specifically characterized group, the family of the young lord—Maud's brother's political ally—who seeks Maud's hand under the brother's sponsorship. The suitor's "old grandfather has lately died" and left a fortune in coal mines to his grandson, a "new-made lord," "first of his noble line," who has a "bought commission" and "gew-gaw castle," "new as his title," built "last year." These details have clear parallels in the family of Tennyson's paternal aunt, Elizabeth Tennyson Russell, who were in close social and political alliance with Charles Tennyson d'Eyncourt. Elizabeth's husband, Major Matthew Russell, inherited from his eighty-year-old father a vast fortune in Durham coal, which he lived to enjoy only five years before leaving it in turn to his own son William and his daughter Emma.[8] Insofar as his family and position are concerned, the grandson–lord in *Maud* is a functional compound of William Russell and Emma's husband, Gustavus-Frederick Hamilton, later Viscount Boyne, who succeeded to the Russell family's property on William's death in 1850, assuming the name and arms of Russell.[9] Tennyson's probable lack of respect for both men makes the identification the more likely.[10] The Russells' Brancepeth Castle was an incredibly expensive and elaborate gingerbread reconstruction which well merited Tennyson's description of the suitor's castle as "pricking a cockney ear over a purple moor." [11] It is no wonder that Elizabeth Russell, after reading *Maud*, sent Tennyson an indignant letter protesting his reflection on her family.[12] Tennyson's apparently sincere denial only bears witness to an astonishing unconsciousness of the autobiographical bearings of his poem.

Postponing for a moment a discussion of the complex

origins in Tennyson's experience of Maud herself, we may pause briefly to consider an aspect of the process by which she became associated in the poem with the surrogates of Tennyson's grandfather and uncle. I have already suggested that Tennyson's memory of Rosa and her family's opposition to his courtship of her played an important part in his creation of Maud. Now Maud's father could stand very well for an Arthur Eden who, like him, was "always in London" and whose "Hall" and daughter were so much like his; but that Eden should be blended with the d'Eyncourts is puzzling until one perceives the autobiographical motive which led to the assimilation. The connection, I believe, lies in the fact that the grandfather and uncle were associated with the failure of Tennyson's courtship of Rosa almost as much as the Edens were. In July, 1835, when Alfred's love for Rosa must have been nearly at its height, old George Tennyson died. Until that event the Somersby family had lived in sanguine expectation that the wealthy old man might do better by them in death than he had done in life. They were bitterly disappointed. Although Alfred's brothers, Frederick and Charles, were left with comfortable incomes, the rest of the family did not receive nearly what they thought their due. Alfred himself, though bequeathed an estate worth about £3000, was furiously angry with his grandfather and with Charles. He denounced his uncle so strongly to his Aunt Mary Bourne, with whom he was staying at Margate, that she felt compelled to send him away from her; and reports of Alfred's outbursts created great resentment in the d'Eyncourt family.[13] Why was Tennyson so angry? Obviously, because his hopes of independence and of leisure for a poetic career had been blasted, but also and more specifically, I believe, because his paltry inheritance made absolutely impossible any thought of marrying Rosa without a great deal more coöperation from her family than there was any reason to expect. Whatever their mutual feelings might be, he had been cut off from her almost irrevocably. Meanwhile his Uncle Charles went happily ahead with the rebuilding of the family seat at Bayons Manor—a home very expensive, no doubt, but absolutely essential to the prominence which the d'Eyncourts had now achieved. The expenditure on the "old place" now "gilt with the hand of a millionaire" must have galled Tennyson very much—enough to weld it in his memory to another Hall which, with Bayons, served as a physical symbol of the barriers which separated him from his beloved.

Equally clear, once the associations just indicated are manifest, is the poetic economy which attached the suitor in the poem to the Russell family. The Russells did not live in Lincolnshire, of course, but one hundred miles to the north in Durham, where Tennyson had never or only very rarely been. Very near Brancepeth Castle, at Whitworth Park, lived Robert Duncombe Shafto—"rich in the graces all women adore"—who married Rosa Baring. Tennyson simply drew from two topographically contiguous and emotionally linked sets of images the material out of which he made the hated suitor of Maud. The close relationship of the Lincolnshire Edens and the Durham Shaftos, together with the equally close relationship of the Lincolnshire d'Eyncourts and the Durham Russells provided the basis of the whole complex of figures in the poem toward which the hero directs his bitter resentment of a selfish and snobbish materialism that, contemptible in his idealistic eyes, has nevertheless the power and will to deprive him of status and of love.[14]

But Maud is more than Rosa, and the story of the speaker's love for Maud is more than the story of Tennyson's love for Rosa. I have begun with these more obvious correspondences in order to establish a ground of presumption upon which to build a more complex but more accurate account of the autobiographical sources and significance of the poem. Before that account can be offered, however, it will be necessary to consider some particulars of Tennyson's early development and of his psychology and philosophy.

II

Very early in his life, in defensive reaction to the terrifying situation of his childhood, Tennyson developed out of the Evangelical creed of his mother two beliefs which remained central to his mature faith: a conviction that ultimate reality was not material but spiritual, and an equally strong persuasion that the central force in the universe was Love.[15] To these doctrines and their corollary, the immortality of the human spirit, he clung desperately, even obsessively, all his life, not simply because he could not face the fact of death and extinction but, much more, because his early religious training, together with the unfortunate family situation and the guilts usual to adolescence, had made it difficult for him to accept the fact of human carnality and sexuality and the whole darker side of human nature which these involved. Tennyson had to believe that man was a spirit in order not to believe that he was a ravening beast. His assumption is plainly inferable from the logic of a famous passage of *In Memoriam:*

And he, shall he,

> Man, her last work, who seem'd so fair,
>   Such splendid purpose in his eyes,
>   Who roll'd the psalm to wintry skies,
> Who built him fanes of fruitless prayer,
>
> Who trusted God was love indeed
>   And love Creation's final law—
>   Tho' Nature, red in tooth and claw
> With ravine, shriek'd against his creed—
>
> Who loved, who suffer'd countless ills,
>   Who battled for the True, the Just,

> Be blown about the desert dust,
> Or seal'd within the iron hills?
>
> No more? A monster then, a dream,
>   A discord. Dragons of the prime,
>   That tare each other in their slime,
> Were mellow music match'd with him.

Tennyson made his point most fully in *Lucretius*, where he represents the philosopher–poet, unknowingly under the influence of an aphrodisiac, as riven by uncontrollable erotic fantasies, "twisted shapes of lust, unspeakable, / Abominable." In the central scene of the poem Lucretius is confronted with the horrifying hallucination of a satyr pursuing a beautiful Oread:

>   but him I proved impossible;
> Twy-natured is no nature; yet he draws
> Nearer and nearer, and I scan him now
> Beastlier than any phantom of his kind
> That ever butted his rough brother–brute
> For lust or lusty blood or provender:
> I hate, abhor, spit, sicken at him; and she
> Loathes him as well; such a precipitate heel,
> Fledged as it were with Mercury's ankle-wing,
> Whirls her to me: but will she fling herself,
> Shameless upon me? Catch her, goat-foot: nay,
> Hide, hide them, million-myrtled wilderness,
> And cavern-shadowing laurels, hide! do I wish—
> What?—that the bush were leafless? or to whelm
> All of them in one massacre? O ye Gods, . . .
> I thought I lived securely as yourselves— . . .
> But now it seems some unseen monster lays
> His vast and filthy hands upon my will,
> Wrenching it backward into his.

Unable to control his animal nature and persuaded by his own materialistic philosophy that the universe offers no possibility of transcendence, Lucretius escapes by taking his own life. The same logic prompted Tennyson himself to say, on many different occasions, that, if he did not believe in immortality, he would commit suicide.[16]

Tennyson's refusal to accept the animal basis of life created in him deeply repressed psychic conflicts which, generating the morbid despondency especially characteristic of his early years, made it difficult for him to sustain his idealistic faith; and his doubts, reinforced as he grew older by the skeptical conclusions of nineteenth-century science, reciprocally intensified the psychic conflicts by weakening the scaffold of rationalization by which he had attempted to surmount them. The result was that his belief suffered from a certain element of strained unreality and he himself from the pressure of emotions which he was unable either to indulge or to suppress.

A complicating side effect of this painful predicament was Tennyson's ambivalent attitude toward the human world around him—his intense desire to be united with and to serve it, and his sense of radical alienation from it. The former sprang out of his loneliness, his need for acceptance, his very idealism; the latter out of the guilty self-consciousness attendant upon his inner stresses, out of the social situation of his semi-ostracized family, out of his bitter awareness and resentment of the spiteful and gossip-ridden community (as it seemed to him at least) in which he lived. Bound by forces he could not understand, stirred by feelings of desire and hate that he could not fully recognize and deal with, he could not extricate himself from the morbid self-centeredness which must have appeared to him as a sinful manifestation of the hereditary "black blood of the Tennysons." [17]

What Tennyson's situation desperately called for was external psychological reinforcement. To take him out of himself, to drain off the poisonous emotion which clogged his spirit, to confirm and vitalize his faith, he needed, quite simply, someone to love and to love him, someone as high-minded as himself, sympathetic, less troubled and more stable. It was the radiant Arthur Hallam, of course, who first and most adequately supplied that need. Hallam's death, when it came, was a blow of overpowering magnitude not only because it meant the loss of a uniquely dear friend but also and primarily because it struck at the basis of the complex psychological and intellectual adjustment which Tennyson had begun to make to the conditions of his own experience. The fact of the death rocked the foundations of his philosophy; the loss of the emotional tie left him isolated, psychologically adrift, at the mercy more than ever of the turbulent forces within him. Before he could be whole again, someone who could take Hallam's place in his spiritual economy had to be found.

Now though Hallam himself had been an object of love and though Tennyson loved him all the more intensely because the relationship was necessarily free of the sensual dangers inherent in a heterosexual relationship,[18] he had, both before and during his friendship with Hallam, continued to see in the love of woman the primary road to spiritual health and salvation. Indeed, Hallam's own neo-Dantean philosophy contributed very extensively to this strain of Tennyson's thought and influenced him profoundly. On the one hand, to be sure, woman might be a seductress, a Vivien or Ettarre, a carnal creature without a soul, to love whom was to submit to the bestial degradation of lust. But—since women, in Merlin's words, differ "as Heaven and Hell"—she might also be (and normatively was) a spiritual being who, through her love, held out to man the possibility of redemption from the toils of the flesh. It was the function of the higher kind of woman, Tennyson says in *The Princess,* to "keep down the base in man" and, in the phrase of an earlier poem, to make "double-natured love lose half its being in [her] spiritual flame." [19] Hallam put the matter succinctly: "Woman's Love was sent / To heal man's tainted heart, and chasten him for Heaven." [20] The angelic woman was in a real sense for Tennyson a savior, a means of grace; in the fact of his love for her, untouched by the baser affections, man, he thought, could find existential evidence of the ultimate spirituality of himself and the universe. Upon that evidence he could build a positive faith adequate to personal affirmation and action.

The "central idea" of *Maud*, Tennyson emphasized in his notes to the poem, is this same "holy power of Love." [21] Hearing Tennyson read *Maud* shortly before his death, Henry Van Dyke was

> amazed at the intensity with which the poet had felt, and the tenacity with which he pursued, the moral meaning of the poem. It was love, but not love in itself alone, as an emotion, an inward experience, a selfish possession, that he was revealing. It was love as a vital force, love as a part of life, love as an influence—nay, *the* influence which rescues the soul from the prison, or the madhouse, of self, and leads it into the larger, saner existence. This was the theme of "Maud." And the poet's voice brought it out, and rang the changes on it, so that it was unmistakable and unforgettable. [22]

The deep personal commitment which, as Van Dyke's remarks make clear, Tennyson had to the thesis of his poem must be understood in terms of the interpenetration of his conception of love, as it emerged from the psycho-biographical background I have described, with the intimate personal relationships of his own life. For Maud—the object of love in the poem—is, I believe, an image in which were blended Tennyson's memories of all three of the women whom he had successively loved—Rosa Baring, Sophy Rawnsley (to an extent), and Emily Sellwood—an image through which he retrospectively defined and interpreted the long search for an ideal and idealizing love which he had carried on from the time of Hallam's death to his marriage with Emily Sellwood.

III

In "O that 'twere possible" we may perceive the clue to the logic of the whole imaginative process involved in the production of the later poem. The lyric—which Tennyson considered the most touching he had ever written [23]—expresses the lament of a lover for a lost love:

> O that 'twere possible
> After long grief and pain
> To find the arms of my true love
> Round me once again!

But the lament is, from a biographical point of view, psychologically ambiguous. On the one hand, like "The Two Voices," "Ulysses," "Tithonus," and the "Morte d'Arthur," written at nearly the same time, the poem undoubtedly derives a great deal of its poignancy from Tennyson's sharp sense of Hallam's loss: [24]

> Ah Christ, that it were possible
> For one short hour to see
> The souls we loved, that they might tell us
> What and where they be.

On the other hand, as a mourning for a woman's love lost, the lyric is less obliquely an expression of need for a kind of love which Tennyson had never yet known, or was only just beginning to know:

> When I was wont to meet her
> In the silent woody places
> By the home that gave me birth,
> We stood tranced in long embraces
> Mixt with kisses sweeter sweeter
> Than anything on earth.

The ambivalence, of course, involves no contradiction but points directly to the complex emotional state in

Tennyson which produced it and tends to confirm what I have already suggested, that the loss of Hallam generated the need for the substitutive love which, in the quick succession of four years, Tennyson sought in Rosa and then in Sophy and Emily. Since all four of the attachments were parallel in potential psychological function and since all four had been, by 1840, successively lost, all four could be represented, in the retrospect of 1854, by the same lyrical lament; they were, in a way, one loss. But the truncated narrative of the early poem could not be filled out, until, with Tennyson's marriage to Emily, the psychic vacuum which produced it had been filled. The writing of *Maud*, then, was no accidental engraftment of a different matter on an alien lyric but a charting in full of the course to which the biographical situation implicit in the earlier poem had led. But this remains to be shown.

The way in which the three women were linked in Tennyson's mind may be inferred from a passage of a very late poem which has an obscure but interesting parallel in *Maud*. In "The Ancient Sage," says Wilfrid Ward (who had discussed the poem at length with Tennyson), "there is much of autobiography," [25] and Tennyson himself said that the "whole poem is very personal." [26] The Sage obviously speaks for the aging poet who shares with him his philosophy, his "Passion of the Past," and his capacity for inducing in himself a mystic state by musing on his own name.[27] The young poet to whom the sage speaks, however, is, to judge from Tennyson's remarks to Ward, in some respects very much like the morbid hero of *Maud*:

> He is dismayed by the first appearance of difficulty and pain in the world, as he had been satisfied for a time with the immediate pleasures within his reach. He is unable to steady the nerve of his brain (so to speak), and trace the riddle of pain and trouble in the universe to its ultimate solution. In thought, as in conduct, he is filled and

100

swayed by the immediate inclination and the first impression, without self-restraint and without the habits of concentrated reflection which go hand in hand with self-restraint. Failing, in consequence, to have any steady view of his own soul or of the spiritual life within, he is impressed, probably by experience, with this one truth, that uncontrolled self-indulgence leads to regret and pain; and he is consequently pessimistic in his ultimate view of things. The absence of spiritual light makes him see only the immediate pain and failure in the universe.[28]

He is, in short, the undisciplined, self-indulgent poet that Tennyson always feared that he himself, without faith, might become—the hero of "The Palace of Art" or of "The Vision of Sin," the "wild poet" of *In Memoriam* who "works / Without a conscience or an aim." He is the Tennyson who might have been, had it not been for the spiritual light of Emily Sellwood. It is this specific point of comparison which illuminates the passage spoken of in *The Ancient Sage*, for a good deal of the young poet's trouble seems to stem from his disappointment in love. He complains, rather cryptically, that

> "The years that when my Youth began
>   Had set the lily and rose
> By all my ways where'er they ran,
>   Have ended mortal foes;
> My rose of love for ever gone,
>   My lily of truth and trust—
> They made her lily and rose in one,
>   And changed her into dust.
> O rosetree planted in my grief,
>   And growing on her tomb,
> Her dust is greening in your leaf,
>   Her blood is in your bloom.
> O slender lily waving there,
>   And laughing back the light,

> In vain you tell me 'Earth is fair'
> When all is dark as night."

The meaning of these lines is not at all clear in the poem, since we are told almost nothing of the young poet's history, but they seem to say that the speaker had been in love with two women of contrasting temperaments, whom he had lost, and then with another, incorporating in some way the qualities of both, who, dying, left him to despair. This meaning is in fact made perfectly clear in a manuscript draft of the passage which, unfortunately, I am not free to quote.[29] The situation referred to, so obscure in the young poet's life, is not obscure in Tennyson's. Rosa Baring was clearly Tennyson's "rose of love," and his warmly affectionate attachment to Sophy ("Lilian") fits a description of her as a "lily of truth and trust"; the nearly simultaneous relationship to both figures (suggested in the manuscript draft) fits what we know of Tennyson's relationship with Rosa and Sophy. The fact that Tennyson's permanent love, Emily Sellwood, ultimately succeeded both in his affections makes her the obvious candidate for the role of "lily and rose in one." Tennyson simply added to his own memories, as befitted the situation of the despairing young poet, the idea of what he might have been had Emily ultimately been lost to him.

Surely it is significant that at the climax of *Maud*, the heroine, who has been identified throughout the poem with the rose (and less extensively with the lily), should become "Queen lily and rose in one." And significant, too, is the fact that just at this point, the hero, cut off, like the poet in "The Ancient Sage," from the woman thus distinctively characterized, falls into despair because of her loss. Such parallels, though inconclusive in themselves, point the way nonetheless to a fruitful biographical analysis of the figure of Maud.

Three associated women in "The Ancient Sage" correspond to three women in Tennyson's life; in *Maud* one woman, I have suggested, stands as a complex fusion of his memories of the same three women. The fusion would be motivated by the already indicated fact that Tennyson's attachments were recurrent attempts to fill the same continuing spiritual need; the contradictions and ambiguities of the poetic relationship, on the other hand, would derive from the fact that, though Tennyson's ultimate motivation remained constant, the actual character of his attachments was quite different—the first springing from passionate infatuation, the second from ethical sympathy, while what might be called his passionately ethical attachment to Emily involved in effect a stabilizing psychological synthesis of the first two. Something of this dialectic (present also in the passage from "The Ancient Sage") underlies, as later I shall try to make clear, the developmental pattern of the hero's feeling for Maud.

Before that, however, it is important to understand that the external circumstances in *Maud* can be related not alone to Rosa but also to Sophy and Emily. I have suggested that "opposition to marriage" (with Rosa) was the associational core of Tennyson's poetic conflation of his grandfather and uncle with Arthur Eden, of the Russells with the Shaftos and of Harrington Hall with Bayons Manor. Other memories also seem to have entered into this complex, on the same principle. Thus, though the dispossession of the hero's father by Maud's is primarily, as I have said, an echo of the disinheritance of Tennyson's own father, the fact that the vague means of dispossession is represented as a swindling commercial scheme—"a vast speculation" —compares with the biographical fact that Tennyson's hopes of an early marriage with Emily were defeated by Dr. Allen's virtual swindle of him in the woodcarving venture, as well as, less directly, by the grandfather's will. (The multiple connection is strengthened by the fact that the invested funds were a legacy from the grandfather and that both his uncle Charles and Emily's father were directly associated in Tennyson's mind with Allen's scheme.) [30] Similarly, one can easily believe that part of the angry emotion directed at Maud's family is an effect of Tennyson's resentment not only of the Edens' opposition to his courtship of Rosa, but also (as Sir Charles thinks) of the opposition of the Sellwood group to his marriage with Emily.[31] The point is that the various elements in the poem have not simple but, as one would expect, complex and overlapping biographical sources. So, for example, though it was Rosa who lived near Tennyson in a Hall, with a father who was "always in London," it was Emily whose mother died in her childhood, and Sophy whose father was Tennyson's father's early friend, as it was she (whom he "watch't with love" from "earliest infancy") of whom he might have said, "I play'd with the girl when a child; she promised then to be fair." But such correspondences are ultimately less significant than those which, as I began to suggest above, relate to the specific character of the hero's attachment to Maud as it may be interpreted by reference to those leading aspects of Tennyson's psychology and philosophy outlined in section ii above.

IV

For the hero of *Maud,* as a psychological critic of the poem has noted, "sex and all physical aspects of human life are identified with nature and rapine," while "his own ego is identified with the absolute ethic and spiritual dignity of orthodox Christianity." [32] The hero looks, sickened, upon a natural world "red in tooth and claw":

> For nature is one with rapine, a harm no
> preacher can heal;
> The Mayfly is torn by the swallow, the spar-
> row spear'd by the shrike,

And the whole little world where I sit is a
  world of plunder and prey.
The same situation obtains in the social world:
  Pickpockets, each hand lusting for all that is
    not its own;
  And lust of gain, in the spirit of Cain, is it
    better or worse
  Than the heart of the citizen hissing in war
    on his own hearthstone.
But the aggression in the world outside the hero is
partly a projection of the conflict within himself, ob-
sessed as he appears in the very first verse of the poem
with "hate" and "blood" and "death." Alienated from
the world by the shock of his father's madness and the
ruthless self-seeking of Maud's family, he is reciprocally
infected by it and, lacking faith in the ultimate meaning of the universe, is powerless to assert his higher
nature against the dark emotions which have poisoned
his soul—"At war with myself and a wretched race, /
Sick, sick to the heart of life, am I."

It is Maud who stirs in him the first faint pulses of
positive feeling. She is, as Rosa must have been to
Tennyson after Hallam's death, a possible source of re-
lease from his spiritual burdens.[33] But Maud's beauty,
the hero feels, may be the "honey of poison flowers"
and involvement with her sensual entrapment. Now
Tennyson apparently came to realize that his own involvement with Rosa was based primarily on sexual attraction, a fact which the ambiguities of his ideal conception of love allowed him for a time to conceal from
himself; and so it is accordingly fruitful to compare the
early stages of the hero's response to Maud with what
little we know of Tennyson's response to Rosa. The
hero views Maud at first as Tennyson came, in his ultimate disillusion, to view his own first love. In Maud's
"perfectly beautiful," "cold and clear-cut face" the hero
sees "dead perfection, no more" ("Faultily faultless,
icily regular, splendidly null"), while Tennyson saw

Rosa as an "icy jewel" whose "perfect-featured face" was "expressionless, / Insipid as the Queen upon a card." [34] Yet the image of her face comes to break the hero's slumber, "growing and fading and growing upon me," just as Tennyson's thoughts had turned to Rosa, "night by night, in musing on thine eyes, / Which look me through when thou art far away."

So, as the hero hears Maud "in the meadow under the Hall," singing "of Death, and of Honour that cannot die," he feels impelled, despite his suspicions, to "move to the meadow and fall before / Her feet on the meadow grass and adore," like the Tennyson who once told Rosa that "my whole heart is vassal at thy feet." But the hero at this point is careful to distinguish between the girl and the feeling her beauty has aroused in him ("Not her, not her, but a voice"), a distinction between projected ideal and objective reality which Tennyson had drawn in "The form, the form alone is eloquent."

All Tennyson's "life and heart and soul" had "tangled" in Rosa's "shining tresses," whereas the suspicious hero fears that with her "sunny hair" Maud may mean to "weave me a snare," to "entangle me," to have "her lion roll in a silken net / And fawn at a victor's feet." Yet, he thinks, if "she were not a cheat, / If Maud were all that she seem'd," then "the world were not so bitter / But a smile could make it sweet."

Drawn by Maud's smile (one remembers Rosa's, "all-perfect"), the hero is soon deeply involved in the ecstatic passion whose extensive and significant association with the rose has been explored in the second chapter. The nature of that passion as represented in the poem may now be more closely examined. The beauty and intensity of the rose–passion lyrics which form the climax of the poem obscure their very definite ambiguity, for the verses clearly indicate that the hero has fallen into the sensual trap of which earlier he had been so wary. In the delirium of love, his blessing is still somehow flawed by a sense of "some dark under-current woe"; but in the garden scene, before the fatal duel, all misgivings are swallowed up by the force of his infatuation:

> She is coming, my own, my sweet;
> Were it ever so airy a tread,
> My heart would hear her and beat,
> Were it earth in an earthy bed;
> My dust would hear her and beat,
> Had I lain for a century dead;
> Would start and tremble under her feet,
> And blossom in purple and red.

Just before this, as the "music clash'd in the hall," the "soul of the rose" had gone into the hero's "blood." It emerges, strangely transformed, in the duel with Maud's brother. The hero's passion for Maud is converted into the aggression which leads him to homicide. "The crime of sense," as Tennyson put it in "The Vision of Sin," has become "the crime of malice." Passionate sexuality, in *Maud* as in *Lucretius*, is identified with the blood–lust of murder; the passion–roses of the garden, as the hero eventually comes to realize, "are not roses but blood." [35] His idealized eroticism has involved him first in an ambiguous passion and then in the violence and hate which spring out of the same animal nature; so that it is with perfect logic that Tennyson places the duel in "the red-ribb'd hollow" where the hero's father had plunged to suicide. There, while a "million horrible bellowing echoes" break, the hero suddenly apprehends the truth. Revolted to find triumphant within himself the very bestial forces which he had feared and hated in the world outside, he falls into a despair more hope-less than ever and calls on God to "strike dead the whole weak race of venomous worms, / That sting each other here in the dust."

Although the dance–duel scene was perhaps asso-ciated in Tennyson's mind with the dance at which he quarreled with both Rosa and Sophy ("lily and rose") and perhaps also with whatever imbroglio with Rosa's family may have stood behind the parallel scenes in "Edwin Morris" and (implicitly) "Locksley Hall," it would be a mistake to suppose that the scene is informed by some particular literal memory and thereby to neglect its larger biographical implication. In the context I have been developing, the duel and its aftermath may be thought of most fruitfully, I think, as Tennyson's symbolic acting out of the aggressions which he had felt toward those who had helped to thwart his love of Rosa and Emily—toward, primarily, his uncle and grandfather and, secondarily, toward the Edens and the Sellwoods. But the scene then also involves his retrospective imaginative judgment on the psychological state which produced those same aggressions—on the ambiguous spiritual development which, in the dark and confused years after the death of his father and of Hallam, had led to his entanglement with Rosa and become merged, in the defeat of his love for her, with the incapacitating and atrophying hatreds which after the loss of her, and of Sophy and Emily, left him progressively more alienated from a society dominated, as it must have seemed to him, by selfish materialism and devoted to scandal and spite.

Rosa's influence, however, is but one strand in the poem. Tennyson had been drawn to her most strongly, we remember, from 1834, shortly after Hallam's death, to 1836, or possibly longer. Nearly at the same period (as the Rawnsleys have it) or perhaps shortly after, he was for a time attracted to Sophy Rawnsley. This attraction, directly contrasting with that to Rosa, was, as I have said, primarily ethical, motivated by Sophy's qualities of mind and spirit. Tennyson was seeking in her (confusedly, as the simultaneous involvement with Rosa would seem to indicate) something which he eventually found fully only in Emily Sellwood, to whom very soon afterwards (in 1838) he became informally engaged. We have in these three closely linked affairs an emotional development oscillating between the two poles of passional and ethical attachment, coming to rest finally at the ethical. It is this essential pattern which is imitated, with much concentration and telescoping, in *Maud*. It is in fact as if, in the part of the poem up to and including the duel, Tennyson had represented his successive and contrasting involvements with Rosa and Emily as a single involvement of double aspect, subsuming the attachment to Sophy in the cognate but much stronger attachment to Emily.[36] For the hero's love of Maud is represented in the poem not only as a possible source of sensual entrapment but also (and ultimately) as a source of spiritual redemption. This aspect of the hero's feeling has its parallel not in Tennyson's infatuation with Rosa or in his mild affection for Sophy but in the intensely tender spiritual rapport that he had known only with Emily Sellwood. It was she, not Rosa or Sophy, who had alone, in those early years and later, effectively raised Tennyson "nearer out of lonely Hell" and made his heart "more blest than heart can tell"; and it is her influence on the poem that we may now more fully examine.

In relation to the psychological-philosophical syndrome with which we have been concerned in interpreting the poem, it is clear that Emily for Tennyson, like Maud for the hero of *Maud*, was the "countercharm of space and hollow sky." In the fact of his innocent love for her he found the inward, spiritual evidence which he set against the doubts generated by the seemingly meaningless world of nineteenth-century science, the

> sad astrology, the boundless plan
> That makes you tyrants in your iron skies,
> Cold fires, yet with power to burn and
> brand
> His nothingness into man.

When he first caught sight of Emily, Tennyson had asked, "Are you an Oread or a Dryad wandering here?"

It was because Emily, like "my Oread" Maud, emerged as a potently spiritual influence that Tennyson could avoid the shattering conclusion about the nature of things which Lucretius's carnal Oread forces him to draw. It was Emily who brought Tennyson's "erring dust" to "fuller orb'd completeness" and she of whom he said, "The peace of God came into my life before the altar when I married her." It was she therefore of whom he might have said that her "gentle will has changed my fate, / And made my life a perfumed altar flame," and she to whom "as long as my life endures / I feel I shall owe . . . a debt, / That I never can hope to pay." Emily had been "my bride to be" and was "my own heart's heart, my ownest own." It was of her, "the noblest woman I have known," and of the bliss-in-prospect before his union with her, therefore, of which he could think as he wrote:

There is none like her, none.
And never yet so warmly ran my blood
And sweetly, on and on
Calming itself to the long-wish'd-for end,
Full to the banks, close on the promis'd good.

But these sentiments, the substance of Tennyson's feeling for Emily at the time of writing as well as in 1838–1840, are, as already indicated, blended in the poem with the quite different sentiments associated with Rosa Baring. This double strand of feeling (represented in the lily and the rose) comes to an end with the dance-duel scene, the correlative, I have suggested, of Tennyson's separation from both women. That he should have represented these in some ways very different separations simultaneously in a single episode is not so puzzling as it might appear. "Represent," in the first place, is much too strong a term, since the correspondence with either separation is in no sense literal and since Tennyson was not intentionally writing biography and must have had only a very cloudy consciousness of the analogy between his own life and the superficially very different story of the poem. What he needed to invent was a functional correlative for his emotion-charged memories, the less obtrusively literal the better; and the single climax of the duel, an artistic necessity in any event, served well enough as a symbolic summing up of all the bitterness of Tennyson's break, in 1837–1840, with Rosa and Emily, as well as with his whole Lincolnshire past. He had been moved toward both women, within a relatively short space of time, by the same deeply rooted psychic need, and he had met two similar and emotively related frustrations. The duel, insofar as it is a conflict with the beloved's family leading to separation, is the literal counterpart of both frustrations and, as already suggested, an acting out of the complex aggressions which Tennyson had directed toward the opponents of both courtships. With the duel Tennyson concluded his concentrated re-creation of the central influences of his early life—the unhappy history of his father, the distresses of his mother, the prolonged antagonism with his uncle and grandfather, the associated animosities toward the Russells, the Edens, the Shaftoes, and the Sellwoods, all of which had lain oppressively on his mind when, like the hero of *Maud,* he took leave of the land of his birth. As the hero emerges from the duel and goes into exile, partly purged of but still troubled and weakened by the old emotional ills, we have a figure who is the poetic counterpart of the chastened but still unstable Tennyson who parted from Emily Sellwood in 1840. The remainder of the poem, a clear but exaggerated analogue of Tennyson's ten-year period of despairing separation from Emily, carries through to full resolution the issues symbolically posed but only partially resolved in the duel.

Who can doubt what experience of his creator lay behind the hero's despairing evaluation of the future prospects of his love—"For years, a measureless ill, / For years, for ever, to part"? Maud, like Emily, unattainable through circumstance and in part estranged, remains a constant symbol of possible redemption: "as long, O God, as she, / Have a grain of love for me," so long "Shall I nurse in my dark heart, / However weary, a spark of will / Not to be trampled out." But despite his hopes of ultimate reunion, the hero, like Tennyson in "Love and Duty," wishes his beloved not to be troubled by him or his memory:

> Me and my harmful love go by;
> But come to her waking, find her asleep,
> Powers of the height, Powers of the deep,
> And comfort her tho' I die.[37]

But Tennyson had been able no more than his hero to sustain himself by what was for both the faintest of hopes. The separation from Emily was, as we have already seen, the crushing climax of a series of frustrations which left him more despondent, more alienated, more unstable than he had ever before been. Try as he might in the succeeding years to forget the past and make a fresh start, he remained powerless to "bury / All this dead body of hate," with serious consequences to his physical and mental health. The madness of the hero may then be read as a melodramatic inflation of Tennyson's mood during the long period of morbid hypochondriacal brooding and water cures that followed his separation from Emily and already traced out in the last chapter. The hero's diatribes against a corrupt society, similarly, are only a heightened version of the bitter railings at the world so often reported in the 'forties by Tennyson's friends.

The manifest correspondence between the last part of the poem and Tennyson's life, though it has apparently struck both Professor Baum and Sir Charles,[38] has not been very generally noted, perhaps because the literal fates of Tennyson and his hero are so different. But this fact should not obscure the very real autobiographical significance of the conclusion. Tennyson could not, of course, marry the hero to Maud because from the outset he had been committed to her death by "O that 'twere possible"; and he had given expression earlier in the poem to the personal feeling for Emily that he felt at the time of writing. What he did in the conclusion was therefore to work out the full logic of the complex psychological development represented in the poem and thus to place the hero in an emotional posture corresponding to that which he himself had come to in marriage with Emily.

Tennyson's love for Emily, so different from his love for Rosa, seems, as I have implied, to have involved in some degree a renunciation and repression of physical sexuality. Tennyson consistently viewed marriage, at its highest, as more a spiritual than a physical communion, and near the end of his life, in the dramatic lyric "Happy," he expressed quite clearly the view which he had from the beginning consistently attempted to sustain:

> The fairest flesh at last is filth on which the
> worm will feast;
> This poor rib-grated dungeon of the holy hu-
> man ghost,
> This house with all its hateful needs no
> cleaner than the beast,
>
> This coarse diseaseful creature which in
> Eden was divine,
> This Satan-haunted ruin, this little city of
> sewers,
> This wall of solid flesh that comes between
> your soul and mine,
> Will vanish and give place to the beauty
> that endures,
>
> The beauty that endures on the Spiritual
> height,
> When we shall stand transfigured, like
> Christ on Hermon hill,

> And moving each to music, soul in soul and
>   light in light,
> Shall flash thro' one another in a moment
>   as we will.

That the hero of *Maud* does not at last possess Maud physically but is only spiritually reunited with her may be seen, therefore, as a symbol of his transcendence of those elements in himself which had caused his long alienation—his latent sensuality and the aggressive hatreds which had been its concomitants. Earlier these passions had been directed toward the roses which "are not roses but blood"; but at the end of the poem the angelic Maud, from her ethereal vantage point, turns them toward a new object:

> She seem'd to divide in a dream from a band
>   of the blest,
> And spoke of a hope for the world in the
>   coming wars—
> "And in that hope, dear soul, let trouble have
>   rest,
> Knowing I tarry for thee," and pointed to
>   Mars
> As he glow'd like a ruddy shield on the Lion's
>   breast.

The ruddiness of Mars is a significant symbolic linkage, for the hero now finally frees himself from alienation by directing his passion, idealized, toward a new kind of rose, "the blood-red blossom of war with a heart of fire." Thus, by sublimation, double-natured love loses half its being and thus the rose of passion merges fully with the lily of ethical love.

Marriage with the "tender, spiritual nature" of Emily meant for Tennyson redemption from the flesh, reunion with the world, enlistment in the wars of active righteousness. Emily, like Edith in "Locksley Hall Sixty Years After," "link'd the broken chain that bound me to my kind"; she, as Maud had done for the hero of *Maud*, drew him "out of the prison . . . of self . . .

into the larger, saner existence." Because of Emily, Tennyson could say, with the hero of *Maud*, "it is time, O passionate heart and morbid eye, / That old hysterical mock-disease should die" (though the hero's is scarcely a mock-disease), and because of her that he could write:

> I have felt with my native land, I am one
> with my kind,
> I embrace the purpose of God and the doom
> assign'd.

Biographically, *Maud* is a crucial document. It is Tennyson's purgative recapitulation of the inner and outer circumstances of his tortured early life, a deeply rooted act of spiritual self-definition and affirmation by which, after the commitment initiated by marriage and the Laureateship, he moved from his earlier to his later career; it is the swan song of the bitter and troubled young poet, the inaugural hymn of the Laureate. Having objectified and judged, as accurately as he was able, the experience of his early life, he felt ready, his own salvation secure, to minister to the moral and spiritual needs of mankind at large. It is therefore no accident that shortly after *Maud* was completed Tennyson began to work on the long-delayed *Idylls of the King;* and it is peculiarly appropriate that "with the proceeds of 'Maud,'" as his son tells us, Farringford—the peaceful home of his later years—"was bought." [39]

V

But *Maud*, which meant so much to the poet who read it so passionately and which contains poetry as lovely and technically perfect as any he wrote, has generally been judged to be an imperfect work of art. Most readers will agree with those critics who, like Mr. Eliot, locate its imperfection in the character of the emotion which flows from the frenetic hero. Distorted and disproportionate to its objects as they appear in the poem, the hero's feeling prevents the reader from identifying with him fully and sympathetically, despite the fact that such identification is almost required by the nature of the poem. On the other hand, the poet does not provide any compensating frame of objectifying judgment by means of which the reader might gain more perspective on the hero and thus a more detached but more understanding and compassionate view of him. The autobiographical reasons for this aesthetically unsatisfactory state of affairs are clear. The feelings Tennyson wished to express in the poem were essentially personal, but, because he could not admit that they were, he had to embody them in an ostensibly dramatic story which would obscure, while it yet remained in formulaic correspondence with, the real private objects of experience which had given it rise. The result was that for him and his speaker the queer disjointed story told in the poem had a hidden emotional dimension which it cannot have for the reader, who must remain perplexed and perhaps annoyed by its insistent and inexplicable manifestation in the poem. The dramatic mask brought still other difficulties: it relieved Tennyson of any moderating sense of responsibility (which otherwise he might have felt) for the exaggerated sentiments expressed, while at the same time, perhaps, it encouraged him to still further exaggeration as a means of convincing himself (and others) that it was after all not he but his distraught hero who spoke.[40] Let the hero rant as he chose, Tennyson in his deep sympathy could still see nothing really out of bounds, so that he was in fact surprised and hurt when others did. (His own intense readings of the poem, significantly, almost always greatly increased his audience's feeling for the hero.)

But this brings us to a more basic point: it was not the fact that the poem was drawn from Tennyson's own experience which caused the trouble but the fact that because he was not emotionally free of that experience he saw it in inadequate perspective. Now poetry, as great poets have told us, is not an expression of subjective emotion but rather an escape from, a transcendence of it; it is the perception in tranquillity of emotions or emotive situations from which the poet is already spiritually free and which he is therefore able to view without loathing or desire; it involves, as Croce saw, a special kind of feeling arising from a detached intuition of the original emotional object.[41] But it is just this emotional precondition of poetry, I think we can see, which is lacking in *Maud*.

Dr. Roy Basler, who carries out an impressive psychological analysis of *Maud* on the assumption that it shows Tennyson's amazingly prescient grasp and objective application of the insights of Freudian psychology, notes that, though the mental illness of the hero is accurately and convincingly elaborated, his recovery is not; the "subtle process of sublimation and reintegration" is not dramatized but rhetorically asserted. "The hero has not in Part III," Dr. Basler goes on, "gained a normal psychic balance, although he (and perhaps the unwary reader) may think he has. He is not completely cured of psychic illness, but has merely exchanged one obsession, self-destruction, for another, self-sacrifice in a noble cause," so that "the problem with which the poem opens is . . . only partly solved at its close." Nevertheless, considering the earlier acuity of the poet's psychological insight, "one cannot suppose that Tennyson was unaware of the irony of his poem's conclusion in effecting the hero's reintegration of personality by means of sublimation and a complete swing from an extreme indulgence in private hysteria to a modified indulgence in public madness."[42] But of course Tennyson was quite unconscious of the irony in the conclusion, for he shared deeply his hero's enthusiasm for the war, believed fervently in the moral efficacy of the public madness,[43] and saw the hero therefore as "raised to sanity by a pure and holy love." [44] Part III—written before the rest of the poem, when the opening of the Crimean War joined with the crisis of Lionel's birth to put Tennyson in an extraordinary emotional situation—was at bottom the poet's own sublimation. His hero's participation in the war was an imaginative projection of his own still unresolved inner conflicts, the "just wrath" directed against the tyrannical Czar a morally acceptable means of releasing by transference his own still deeply repressed aggressions.[45] Since he was then still held by the psychic forces which had controlled the process of experience represented in the poem—still (though less obviously) at war with himself and a wretched race— in constructing the work he was unable to contemplate or recreate that experience without emotional distortion and hence aesthetic imperfection.

All this, of course, was not a merely mechanical effect of Tennyson's psychological situation but depended as well on his more conscious relation to the materials of the poem. Even while his spiritual problems remained unresolved he might have managed either to leave them unexpressed or at least to see in clearer rational perspective, or with some degree of irony, the circumstances in his early life out of which they had grown. But that would have required more knowledge of himself than he was able or willing to achieve, a conscious recognition of the real nature of his grievances which would perhaps have involved a greater shock than his delicately balanced spirit could bear. He could not bring his troubles fully to his own and to public judgment because, as in some part of his mind he must have known, they would not stand inspection. But neither, so insistent was their pressure, could he put them behind him and leave them unexpressed. The solution to his dilemma—perhaps after all the only solution possible for him—was the imperfect *Maud*.

The weakness of *Maud* illuminates parallel problems of poetic personality in a substantial body of

Tennyson's later (and earlier) work, for at the deepest psychological level he never moved beyond the end of *Maud*. Though he continued to sublimate his spiritual burdens in high-minded crusades for Right and Truth, such means were not fully adequate to cleanse his bosom of the stuff which weighed upon his heart, so that they had to be indulged in, as *Maud* had to be rehearsed, again and again. He had embraced the purpose of God, the doom assigned; he had kissed the ideal rod his own moral will had wrought. But he had not really succeeded in becoming one with his kind, nor did he ever achieve full perception of or genuine empathy with the real world of men as it lay outside the immediate circle of his acquaintance. He lived out his life at his Farringford and Aldworth retreats, isolated if no longer wholly alienated, remote from the main stream of intellectual life, and sunk, as FitzGerald perhaps too unkindly put it, "in coterie worship, and (I tremble to say it) in the sympathy of his most ladylike, gentle wife." [46] With Emily at Farringford Tennyson found peace, but it was an armed peace. The skinned ulcer in his soul continued to fester and broke out during the later years in many ways—in occasional fits of depression, in complaints about the past and present, in hysterical attacks on the forces of evil (socialism, free-thinking, revolution, the new realism in literature), forces which threatened from without the citadel of idealism he had built on not altogether solid psychological ground within. The old mock-disease, not really dead, continued to infect his poetry (most notably, perhaps, the overly gorgeous, shrilly emotional *Idylls of the King*,[47] where the sensually beautiful Guinevere grovels at the feet of the spiritual Arthur), as Tennyson continued his blind struggle with the problems which, posed by his early life, he had tried but failed to solve in *Maud*. "He mastered circumstances," his dear friend Jowett said of him, "but he was also partly mastered by them"; [48] to the extent that he *was* mastered by circumstances, much of his poetry, despite its lyrical brilliance and technical finish, is necessarily prevented from being poetry of the very first rank.

But in recognizing and defining through *Maud* the sources of Tennyson's poetical deficiencies, we can also perceive more clearly some of the reasons for the success of that very substantial part of his work which is indubitably and enduringly great. It is only apparently paradoxical, to take the chief instance, that *In Memoriam,* his greatest poem, should, like *Maud,* draw upon his own immediately personal experience. Despite the poignancy of Tennyson's lament and the consistently personal point of view maintained throughout, *In Memoriam* is aesthetically, in contrast to the outwardly dramatic but really subjective *Maud,* a very objective poem. Coventry Patmore once demonstrated to a reluctant Aubrey de Vere that Tennyson's elegies "each and all contained indications of consciousness, artifice, and other qualities inconsistent with the existence of any very lively flow of feeling at the time of writing"; [49] but Patmore's accurate analysis was less damning than he supposed. Tennyson himself indeed agreed with Patmore's judgment. *In Memoriam,* he told James Knowles, "is a very impersonal poem as well as personal"; "it is rather the cry of the whole human race than mine" [50]—which was Tennyson's way of saying that he was free, in writing the poem, of any oppressive burden of immediately subjective feeling; his grief was, as it were, recollected in tranquillity. And therein lies the source of the extraordinary lucidity and serenity of feeling in the poem. *In Memoriam* is a spiritual record of those years in Tennyson's life which eventually found another, more covert record in *Maud;* but the first poem, unlike the second so long delayed, involved no feeling which Tennyson could not contemplate with equanimity and come to clear and conscious terms with; and so, writing over the whole extent of those years, in moments as I believe of spiritual freedom and quietude, he could give to his best private feeling full and appropriate public expression, while his more ambivalent and less conscious emotions remained in uneasy suspension until the crisis of success forced their unsatisfactory discharge in *Maud*.

The comparison instructs us to look for Tennyson's supremacy, not in those poems where he was sublimating his inner frustrations or moralizing out of the wisdom born of the Pyrrhic victories that one part of his divided soul had gained over the other, but rather in those where, in full spiritual equilibrium, he spoke in the untroubled voice of his mature being. This is not to say that *Maud*—or "Locksley Hall" or the *Idylls*— are anything less than what they clearly are, the unmistakable work of a major poet; it is to say that Tennyson's unconditional poetic success came only in those many poems (I think particularly of the lovely and too much ignored verses of occasion, of celebration, greeting, and elegy) where, as in *In Memoriam*, he speaks not as dark romantic or ancient sage but with the perfect clarity, tact, and grace of the great classical poet that in the truest part of him he was.

Notes

CHAPTER 1.

[1] Mrs. Carlyle's remarks are conveniently collected in Charles R. Saunders, "Carlyle and Tennyson," *PMLA*, LXXVI (March, 1961), 91–92.

[2] See Sir Charles Tennyson, *Alfred Tennyson* (London, 1949), p. 524. Sir Charles has inadvertently placed the reading in September, 1891, whereas it actually took place in late August, 1892. See Van Dyke's "The Voice of Tennyson," *Century Magazine*, XLV (Feb., 1893), 539, 544.

[3] *Alfred Tennyson*, pp. 289 and 396.

[4] Hallam Lord Tennyson, *Alfred Lord Tennyson: A Memoir by His Son* (London, 1897), II, 409.

[5] *Memoir*, I, 378–379.

[6] *Works*, ed. Hallam Lord Tennyson (London, 1913), p. 958.

[7] *Tennyson and His Friends*, ed. Hallam Lord Tennyson (London, 1911), pp. 308–309.

[8] All these accounts were written years after the event, Tennyson's when he was working with his son on the final edition of his poems, de Vere's and Mrs. Ward's after the poet's death. In addition, we must remember that Mrs. Ward had her information at second hand and that the memories of all the informants must have been influenced by forty years of anecdote and reminiscence.

[9] In H. D. Rawnsley, *Memories of the Tennysons*, 2nd ed. (Glasgow, 1912), pp. 123–124. Rawnsley does not date this interview precisely, but it seems to have taken place in 1852 or 1853. The story is supported by the presence, in the Rawnsley portion of the Tennyson papers at Harvard, of a complete manuscript of the 1837 "Stanzas," though it is not in Tennyson's hand (Harvard bMS Eng 952.2, No. 28). Rawnsley could not easily have seen Mrs. Ward's account when he wrote, but he must have seen de Vere's in the *Memoir*.

[10] M. L. Howe, "Dante Gabriel Rossetti's Comments on *Maud*," *MLN*, XLIX (May, 1934), 291.

[11] See Joyce Green, "Tennyson's Development During the 'Ten Years' Silence' (1832–1842)," *PMLA*, LXVI (Sept., 1951), 671.

[12] This letter, now in the library of Trinity College, Cambridge, has been published in James Pope-Hennessy, *Monckton Milnes: The Years of Promise, 1809–1851* (London, 1949), p. 93.

[13] Harvard MS Eng 952, No. 21, p. 24; the 1837 version is described and quoted by Thomas R. Lounsbury, *The Life and Times of Tennyson* (New Haven, 1915), pp. 273 ff.

[14] Mrs. Ward, in the *Memoir*, I, 377.

[15] The date is definitely established by Tennyson's reference to it in an unpublished letter to Sophy Rawnsley Elmhirst (dated June 8, 1854), now in the Duke University Library; and by an entry in Emily Tennyson's slightly less reliable manuscript journal (see n. 20), which records both the christening and the Simeon visit.

[16] Unpublished. Harvard MS Eng 952.1, No. 145. Quoted by permission of Harvard College Library.

[17] *Memoir*, I, 405.

[18] Basil Champneys, *Memoirs and Correspondence of Coventry Patmore* (London, 1900), II, 305.

[19] "The war is only an episode," Tennyson told Van Dyke ("The Voice of Tennyson," p. 539).

[20] Reference is to the *manuscript* of Emily's journal, which Sir Charles Tennyson has kindly allowed me to see; but cf. *Memoir*, I, 372, and *Works*, p. 959. The manuscript journal should be distinguished from the printed extracts from it which appear in the *Memoir* and in Hallam Tennyson's printed but not published *Materials for a Life of A. T.* (4 vols.), because Hallam edited his quotations from it rather liberally before printing. But the manuscript journal itself must not be taken as contemporary material, since, as Sir Charles informs me, it represents a redaction made late in life by Emily (with the help of Hallam) from the original journal, which was then destroyed as too personal for preservation. The entries printed in Hallam's biographical works as from Emily's journal, then, are redactions of a redaction of the actual journal.

[21] Quotations are from the *Morning Chronicle*, March 13, 1854, but their like are to be found in the *Times* as well. There are other, less striking echoes which I do not note. I think no one could read the papers of these days and Part III together without coming to feel that Tennyson wrote under their influence.

[22] The first was written in the "early thirties" (Sir Charles Tennyson, *Alfred Tennyson*, p. 281), and F. T. Palgrave records hearing the second in summer of 1853 (*Memoir*, II, 504, and I, 363). (Mr. Christopher Ricks tells me that he has seen "Go Not Happy Day" in a MS collection for *The Princess* dating from 1849.)

[23] "In April the diary says that he drew my mother out in her garden chair to see the 'wealth of daffodils' and the ruby sheaths of the lime leaves" (*Memoir*, I, 374).

[24] In February, 1855, when *Maud* was almost fully completed, Tennyson wrote the famous "mad scene," which he then inserted between "O that 'twere possible" and Part III, thus making the transition between the two less abrupt (*Materials for a Life of A. T.*, II, 108).

[25] *Memoir*, II, 493.

[26] Sir Charles Tennyson has called my attention both to the passage and its implication: "Nov. 1ˢᵗ Mʳ Moxon comes & when told that friends wanted the Poems now nearly ready for publication to be published at once he kindly urged that they should be regardless of trouble to himself & left next day." The "Poems" referred to were almost certainly *Maud*, but, since the *Memoir* records that Tennyson continued to work on the poem well into 1855, he must in November have had in view a shorter version than that which he eventually published.

[27] See *Memoir*, I, 376–377.

[28] *Memoir*, I, 377.

[29] In addition to the letters he quotes, Hallam Tennyson says of the period only that Tennyson's "overwhelming sorrow . . . as my father told me, for a while blotted out all joy from his life, and made him long for death, in spite of his feeling that he was in some measure a help and comfort to his sister," and, some pages on, that "after a period of utter prostration from grief, and many dark fits of blank despondency," "his passionate love of truth, of nature, and of humanity, drove him to work again, with a deeper and fuller insight into the requirements of the age" (*Memoir*, I, 109 and 123).

[30] Bodleian MS Eng. misc. e. 351, foll. 15ʳ–16ʳ.

[31] Fol. 21ᵛ.

[32] Oct. 28, 1833; Lincolnshire Archives Office (hereafter abbreviated as L.A.O.) T d'E. H/113/51.

[33] The two poems are dated October 6 and October 20, respectively, in the Heath Commonplace Book. See Green, p. 670.

[34] James Knowles, "Aspects of Tennyson, II: (A Personal Reminiscence)," *Nineteenth Century*, XXXIII (Jan., 1893), 182.

[35] *Memoir*, I, 109.

[36] *Letters of Edward FitzGerald*, ed. W. A. Wright (London, 1907), I, 25. Wright gives the date of the letter in brackets, which has perhaps made scholars hesitate to draw the obvious inference, but A. McKinley Terhune kindly informs me that the date of the letter is determinable from the postmark on the accompanying envelope.

[37] See Mary Joan Ellmann, "Tennyson: Unpublished Letters, 1833–36," *MLN*, LXV (April, 1950), 224; the related letters in the *Memoir*, I, 128–131; and the letter from Tennant quoted immediately below.

[38] *Memoir*, I, 498. Years afterward Tennyson remembered himself in these early days as "utterly miserable, a burden to myself and to my family" (*Memoir*, I, 193, n. 2).

[39] Rashdall says that the girl was "a daughter of the authoress of 'Domestic Manners of the Americans.'" This would have been Cecilia Trollope, who was visiting her relatives, the Trollopes of Harrington Rectory, near Somersby (L. P. and R. P. Stebbins, *The Trollopes: The Chronicle of a Writing Family* [New York, 1945], pp. 58–59).

[40] Fol. 28ᵛ.

[41] The day after the party at the Brackenbury's Clara Tennyson,

Julia's sister, reported to brother George that "poor Emily" had "not at all recovered the shock she received from Hallam's death." "This was indeed," she continued, "a melancholy thing" (L.A.O. T d'E. H/113/61). Emily was not, of course, at the Brackenbury party and, as nearly as one can tell from the surviving records, did not go out socially at all.

[42] To Spring Rice, mid-November (Ellmann, p. 224); to J. M. Kemble, late November or early December (*Memoir*, I, 130–131); and to R. M. Milnes, December 3 (*Memoir*, I, 132). Earlier, apparently, his letters had been less cheerful, for on November 26, Francis Garden wrote to R. C. Trench: "When in London I saw a letter from poor Alfred Tennyson. Both himself and his family seemed plunged in the deepest affliction" (*Memoir*, I, 107).

[43] *Memoir*, I, 131.

[44] L.A.O. T d'E. H/113/67. Since Alfred's attitude toward publication at this time is of some interest, I give the rest of Frederick's remarks on the subject here: "I forget," he continues, "whether his second volume had appeared before you left England. I hold it to be considerably superior to the first. Though some blackguard wrote a filthy thing against him in the Quarterly this has merely had the effect of promoting the sale of the book." It is difficult to know what to make of this. The review did not promote the sale of the book (*Alfred Tennyson*, p. 137); and whatever Tennyson's attitude toward publication may have been in late 1833, it was not favorable in the spring of 1835, when he wrote to Spedding: *"I do not wish to be dragged forward again in any shape before the reading public at present,* particularly on the score of my old poems" (*Memoir*, I, 145). But since Frederick repeats his assertion in his letter of February 10 and since Hallam Tennyson's statement that Tennyson refused to publish in the fall of 1834 is based upon a misinterpretation of the same letter, it is just as well to recognize that no contemporary evidence earlier than the letter to Spedding (late March, 1835) can be set against Frederick's declaration in support of the usual view that the resolution which produced the famous ten years' silence was an immediate effect of the *Quarterly* review and/or Hallam's death.

[45] Fol. 35ᵛ.

[46] *Memoir*, I, 106.

[47] Fol. 36ᵛ.

[48] Fol. 38ʳ.

[49] *Memoir*, I, 109. The place of this undated passage in Hallam Tennyson's narrative suggests that he attributed it to the period immediately succeeding Hallam's death, but it seems more likely that Tennant would have written thus after his January visit, for in November Alfred's mood had appeared to him unrelievedly bitter.

[50] Fol. 39ʳ.

[51] No. LXXXV was one of the first written of the *In Memoriam* elegies (*Memoir*, I, 109), but Mrs. Ellmann has pointed out that the early version in the Heath Commonplace Book omits this and other stanzas of the published poem ("Tennyson: Revision of *In Memoriam*, Section 85," *MLN*, LXV [Jan., 1950], 27).

[52] L.A.O. T d'E. H/116/9.

[53] Fol. 42^r.

[54] *Alfred Tennyson,* p. 150.

[55] *Works,* p. 954. Henry Hallam's undated letter of request (*Memoir,* I, 108) must have come at the end of January, for Tennant records the receipt of a similar letter on January 28. See *Letters to Frederick Tennyson,* ed. Hugh J. Schonfield (London, 1930), p. 35.

[56] *Alfred Tennyson,* p. 151.

[57] Quoted from the original letter to John Frere in the Duke University Library. Hallam Tennyson has used this letter very carelessly in constructing a passage in the *Memoir* which has commonly been used to establish Tennyson's state of mind and attitude toward publication in the fall of 1834 (to which period Hallam attributes the letter). He writes (I, 138): "The elder brother Frederick was just then in the midst of music at Milan. He wrote a few lines urging my father to publish in the spring. But he would not and could not; his health since Hallam's death had been 'variable and his spirits indifferent.'" Obviously, Hallam has (1) misdated the letter by approximately eight months, despite Frederick's clear superscription "Somersby February 10th 1834," and moved him prematurely to Italy from Lincolnshire; (2) converted Frederick's statement that Alfred *would* publish to an implied statement by Alfred that he would *not;* and (3) attributed Frederick's phrase about Alfred's variable spirits implicitly to Alfred himself and unjustifiably given it specific association with Hallam's death.

[58] Letter from Clara Tennyson to George Hildeyard Tennyson (April 27, 1834); L.A.O. T d'E. H/116/22.

[59] See *Memoir,* I, 124, and *Alfred Tennyson,* p. 149, but also Jerome H. Buckley, *Tennyson: The Growth of a Poet* (Cambridge, Mass., 1960), p. 68 and p. 270, n. 13.

[60] Fol. 42^r.

[61] L.A.O. T d'E. H/116/18.

[62] L.A.O. T d'E. H/116/19.

[63] Fol. 45^r.

[64] Sir Charles (*Alfred Tennyson,* p. 151) places the letter in early summer. It seems likely from a reference in Tennyson's letter of August 21 that it was sent in late June, before his visit to the Heaths and Hallams.

[65] That Tennyson at this time visited the Hallams as well as the Heaths has apparently gone unnoticed by the biographers. In a letter to his grandfather dated from Somersby, August 21, 1834, Alfred says that he has "been spending the last four weeks at Mr Serjeant Heath's house near Dorking & with the Hallams at Moulsey-Park near Kingston" (L.A.O. T d'E. H/147/11). He must have gone to the Hallams first, for the letters he received at the Heaths in mid-July from Emily and his mother (*Memoir,* I, 135–136) imply that he had just transmitted to Emily an invitation from the Hallams to visit. Alfred's mood during his stay with the Heaths is suggested by some light verses he wrote at the time (Buckley, p. 69).

[66] This is uncertain. Alfred's August 21 letter says that he has been

127

away the "last four weeks," but Hallam Tennyson prints a letter from Tennant, dated August 4 (*Memoir*, I, 137), which implies that he had been at Somersby and had received a letter from Alfred since; so that on this evidence Tennyson must have returned home nearly a month before he wrote his grandfather, a conclusion which would agree with the implication of Emily's July 12 letter that he had already been with the Hallams and would leave the Heaths in less than three weeks. Tennant's letter, however, is dated only "1834" in Hallam Tennyson's unpublished *Materials for a Life of A.T.* and is there printed with another, purportedly earlier letter, proposing the visit, dated October 25, 1834 (I, 160–161), so that Hallam may well have obscured the sequence of events; but since Alfred in his August letter is apologizing for neglecting a prior letter of his grandfather's, a simpler explanation would be that his statement reflects his disinclination to call the old man's attention to the time which had elapsed since his return.

[67] The time of this arrangement is also uncertain because of the confusion in the dates of Tennant's letters, but Hallam Tennyson's statement (*Memoir*, I, 137) that a sympathetic and practical Tennyson concocted the plan of Horatio's schooling in August in order to encourage Tennant, as well as to help his academically lagging brother, is certainly erroneous. The plan was originated months before, during Tennant's January visit, and was largely due to Tennant himself (see *Letters to Frederick Tennyson*, pp. 33–37).

[68] According to the letters Emily and Alfred's mother wrote him in mid-July (*Memoir*, I, 135–136), Emily was to travel to the Hallams with Charles "in about three weeks' time," but apparently Emily's wish to be introduced to the Hallams by Alfred resulted in a postponement. Sir Charles says that Tennyson took Emily to the Hallams in September, at the same time that he took Horatio to Tennant (*Alfred Tennyson*, p. 151), but a more likely date would be October. In a letter which is a reply to one of Spedding's dated September 19, 1834, Tennyson says, "I am going to town with Emily tomorrow," and since he also says that Spedding has "waited some time for a reply," it seems unlikely that his letter (dated only 1834 in the *Memoir*, I, 140) was written in September, especially since Spedding's letter had been sent through an intermediary.

[69] H. D. Rawnsley, *Memories of the Tennysons* (Glasgow, 1912), p. 65.

[70] Fol. 48ᵛ. By chance we have another record of this party in a letter from Tennyson's cousin Louis to his father (Nov. 11, 1834; L.A.O. T d'E. H/115/36). Louis, like the rest of the d'Eyncourts, rather shrank from his Somersby cousins, as the letter indicates: "Yesterday week I went with Charles to a dance at Somersby. I excused myself at first on the ground that I could not leave my Mother —Charles mentioned it to her, & she kindly & unadvisedly s[ai]d she did not want me to stay, so that my excuse was gone, & not liking to have recourse to another, lest Charles sh[oul]d think I was determined not to go I went:—My aunt received me most kindly— There was a very pleasant party there of the country neighbours."

[71] For an account of Tennyson's poetic activity in this period see Miss Green's article, pp. 669–674. (See above, n. 11.)

[72] See above, n. 44.

[73] From the time of his visit to Spedding, in the spring of 1835, till the spring of 1838, there is almost no reference to Alfred in the papers of his friends; and only three or four letters of his have, so far as I know, survived from this period. His poetic production is difficult to gauge, but most of the new poems in the 1842 volumes are associated with the burgeoning of 1834 or with the post-1838 period; cf. *Alfred Tennyson*, p. 168.

CHAPTER 2.

[1] In 1923, for instance, Sir Harold Nicolson wrote: "And, indeed, we are assured by Canon Rawnsley that 'Thy rosy lips are soft and sweet' was addressed to Rosa Baring. And that 'Airy fairy Lilian' is to be identified as Sophy Rawnsley. All of which was, and is, of no importance either to Tennyson or to ourselves" (*Tennyson: Aspects of His Life, Character and Poetry* [London, 1949 reprint], p. 43).

[2] Sir Charles Tennyson, *Alfred Tennyson* (London, 1949), pp. 162–163.

[3] Sir Charles Tennyson, *Six Tennyson Essays* (London, 1954), p. 102. More recently still Sir Charles has said that "there is little doubt that Tennyson was in the early 1830's seriously in love with Rosa Baring, stepdaughter of the then tenant of Harrington, whose family were unfavourable to his suit" ("Alfred Tennyson and Somersby," *The Tennyson Chronicle*, X (August, 1959), [9].

[4] For Sir Francis Baring, see the *DNB* and the obituary in the *Gentleman's Magazine*, LXXX:ii (Sept., 1810), 293; for his descendants, see *Burke's Peerage, sub* Northbrook, and the accounts of the various prominent members of the family also in the *DNB*.

[5] See Ralph W. Hidy, *The House of Baring in American Trade and Finance* (Cambridge, Mass., 1949), p. 44.

[6] *Proceedings of the Dorset Natural History and Antiquarian Field Club*, ed. Herbert Pentin (Dorchester, 1906), XXVII, xliv.

[7] *Gentleman's Magazine*, XC:ii (July, 1820), 94.

[8] See *Burke's Peerage, sub* Sydenham, and the articles on Sydenham (Charles Edward Poulett Thomson) and his brother, George Poulett Scrope, in the *DNB*.

[9] For the Eden family see *Burke's Peerage, sub* Auckland.

[10] Letter from Arthur Eden's mother to Lord Auckland, British Museum Add. MS 34, 455, f. 357.

[11] The mistake was originated, curiously enough, by W. F. Rawnsley (*Tennyson and His Friends*, ed. Hallam Lord Tennyson [London, 1911], pp. 21 and 25), whose brother was named after Arthur Eden (see *Burke's Landed Gentry, sub* Rawnsley of Well Vale).

[12] Letter from Eden to Lord Brougham, Aug. 14, 1851, now in the University College Library.

[13] W. D. Paden, *Tennyson in Egypt* (Lawrence, Kansas, 1942), p. 120 n.

[14] This is manifest from Rashdall's and Massingberd's diaries (see below).

[15] H. D. Rawnsley, *Memories of the Tennysons*, 2nd ed. (Glasgow, 1912), p. 63.

[16] Bodleian MS Eng. misc. e. 351, foll. 23^r–24^v.

[17] Lincolnshire Archives Office, Mass. 8/1, pp. 85–86 and 96.

[18] I have been unable to locate any record of Rosa's birth; but since her parents were married in 1810, she, the youngest of three daughters, could not have been born earlier than 1813; and W. F. Rawnsley ("Personal Recollections of Tennyson," *Nineteenth Century and After*, XCVII [Feb., 1925], 192) knew her when she was eighty-four, so that, since she died in 1898, she could have been born no later than 1814.

[19] The portrait, now in the Shafto home at Whitworth Park, Durham, is reproduced in the periodical version of this chapter, "Tennyson and Rosa Baring," *Victorian Studies*, V (March, 1962), 233.

[20] The verses appear in Rosa's birthday book, described below.

[21] See Sir Timothy Eden, *Durham* (London, 1952), II, 399.

[22] See *Burke's Landed Gentry, sub* Shafto of Whitworth.

[23] *Memories*, p. 63.

[24] This is indicated clearly enough by W. F. Rawnsley in his essay in *Tennyson and His Friends* (pp. 21 and 25) and by the papers of the Shaftoes and Massingberds, cited above. Various poems of H. D. Rawnsley appear in Rosa's birthday book, seeming to indicate that he himself knew Rosa for some years.

[25] *Memories*, pp. 63–64.

[26] *Ibid.*, pp. 67–68. The autograph in the birthday book bears no title. The poem is written on both sides of one sheet of paper; Rosa has inadvertently trimmed off most of the first words of the lines of the first section in fitting it within an engraved rule on the birthday book page.

[27] *Alfred Tennyson*, p. 143.

[28] *Memories*, p. 64. No autograph of this poem appears in the birthday book, but a copy of it (undated) is there marked in Rosa's hand "Alfred Tennyson" and "To Rosa Baring." Among the Rawnsley portion of the Tennyson papers at Harvard are typed copies of all the poems which appear in *Memories;* these are apparently those which Rosa gave to Rawnsley's mother (*Memories*, p. 68 n.). The typed copy of "Thy rosy lips" (Harvard bMS Eng 952.2, No. 30) is headed "To Rosa Baring / On her Birthday / 1834." Rosa's birthday was September 23.

[29] A copy of the poem in Palgrave's handwriting is tipped into his copy of Tennyson's 1853 *Poems* (now in the British Museum) with the inscription; "Recited by him to me at Farringford: in 1854." An untitled copy of the same verses is among the Tennyson papers at Harvard (bMS Eng 952.1, No. 120).

[30] The poem is printed in this form in Hallam Tennyson's *Alfred Lord Tennyson: A Memoir* (London, 1897), II, 311–312, with the comment that in 1885 Tennyson sent it to a friend for publication in a volume titled *Ros Rosarum;* but a draft of the poem, which I am

not permitted to quote, appears in an early composition book (o.15.21 in the Tennyson collection at Trinity College, Cambridge [hereafter abbreviated as T.C.]) with "Tithon" and "O that 'twere possible," both of which date from 1833–1834. See Mary Joan Donahue, "Tennyson's Hail, Briton! and *Tithon* in the Heath Manuscript," *PMLA,* LXIV (June, 1949), 400; and Joyce Green, "Tennyson's Development During the 'Ten Years' Silence' (1832–1842)," *PMLA,* LXVI (Sept., 1951), 671. Tennyson said in 1860 that "Tithonus" had been "written upwards of a quarter of a century ago" (*Works,* ed. Hallam Lord Tennyson, single-volume edition [London, 1913], p. 916).

[31] Tennyson's autograph in Rosa's birthday book is undated, but Rosa has recopied the poem and dated it "1835," though the "5" might easily be mistaken for a "6." In the typed Harvard copy (bMS Eng 952.2, No. 29), which may also have authority from Rosa (see n. 28), the poem is marked "1836," the date Rawnsley gives it in his *Memories.*

[32] Shafto's obituary appeared in the *Times* for March 25, 1889, p. 9 f.

[33] In structure and psychic mechanism, the poem is very like "In the Valley of Cauteretz."

[34] *Unpublished Early Poems by Alfred Tennyson,* ed. Sir Charles Tennyson (London, 1931), pp. 63–64.

[35] "I lingered" exists in three versions in the Harvard Tennyson papers (bMS Eng 952, No. 8, p. 12; 952.1, Nos. 20 and 93), the earliest watermarked 1835, the latest 1836; "Ah, fade not yet" exists in two MSS (bMS Eng 952.1, Nos. 1 and 57), but only one of these is watermarked and the date does not appear. The earlier version, however, appears on the reverse of a leaf bearing "How thought you that this thing could captivate" (see below), a later version of which appears, with the "Bridesmaid" sonnet and "I lingered" on a double leaf watermarked 1836; so that both sonnets clearly belong to the period 1835–1836.

[36] This is Sir Charles' opinion (*Alfred Tennyson,* p. 163).

[37] *Unpublished Early Poems,* p. 77.

[38] This is one of three poems which, though written in "early life," were not published till 1865 (*Works,* p. 900), when they appeared as "Three Sonnets to a Coquette":

> The form, the form alone is eloquent!
> A nobler yearning never broke her rest
> Than but to dance and sing, be gaily drest,
> And win all eyes with all accomplishment:
> Yet in the whirling dances as we went,
> My fancy made me for a moment blest
> To find my heart so near the beauteous breast
> That once had power to rob it of content.
> A moment came the tenderness of tears,
> The phantom of a wish that once could move,
> A ghost of passion that no smiles restore—
> For ah! the slight coquette, she cannot love,
> And if you kissed her feet a thousand years,
> She still would take the praise, and care no more.

Nothing but my intuition connects this poem with Rosa; but it must certainly have been written about a real woman, and there are no other candidates. I should record here too my guess that "Come Not When I Am Dead" and "The Letters," published respectively in 1851 and 1855, also have some reference to Rosa, the first for reasons which, considering my argument below, are obvious; the second because of its not quite dramatically self-contained subject matter and because of its reference to a vane and a tower and other (topographical) features which fit Harrington Hall and the Harrington–Somersby neighborhood.

[39] The poem is given in the *Memories*, p. 65; Tennyson's autograph in the birthday book is undated, but the typed copy (Harvard bMS Eng 952.2, No. 30) is labeled "1836," which date is given by Rawnsley. Rosa's birthday, again, was September 23. The poem runs:

> Thy natal day awakens bright,
> Once more that happy morn doth rise
> Wherein thine eyes first saw the light
> And light grew lighter for thine eyes.
> So let the varying moments flee,
> And, passing, change us less or more,
> Whilst time himself, in love with thee,
> But makes thee lovelier than before.

[40] Something of the reaction Tennyson must have engendered in the neighbors round can be divined by reading between the lines of Rosa's reminiscences and Sophy Elmhirst's (*Memories*, pp. 68 ff.).

[41] Quoted by Thomas R. Lounsbury, *The Life and Times of Tennyson* (New Haven, 1915), p. 444.

[42] *Tennyson and His Friends*, pp. 269–270.

[43] These are Hallam Tennyson's words (*Memoir*, II, 379); Tennyson said that " 'Locksley Hall' is an imaginary place (tho' the coast is Lincolnshire) and the hero is imaginary. The whole poem represents young life, its good side, its deficiencies, and its yearnings" (*Memoir*, I, 195).

[44] *Memoir*, II, 331.

[45] *Memoir*, I, 401–402; cf. *Memoir*, II, 329–330.

[46] See Douglas Bush's introduction to his selections from Tennyson in *Major British Writers*, enlarged edition (New York, 1959), II, 369; and H. M. McLuhan's introduction to *Alfred Lord Tennyson: Selected Poetry* (New York, 1956), p. v.

[47] Amy Woolner, *Thomas Woolner, R. A.: His Life in Letters* (New York, 1917), pp. 218–225, gives in full the story on which the poem is based.

[48] *Memoir*, II, 9.

[49] J. H. Buckley, *Tennyson: The Growth of a Poet* (Cambridge, Mass., 1960), p. 76.

[50] "Tennyson's *Locksley Hall* and Thomas Carlyle," in *Booker Memorial Studies*, ed. Hill Shine (Chapel Hill, 1950), p. 57.

[51] So I am informed by the Reference Department of the Yale University Library, where the manuscript, given by Tennyson to Frederick Tuckerman in 1855 (*Alfred Tennyson*, p. 284), is now preserved.

[52] *Memoir*, I, 162.

[53] Lushington's recollection, omitted from the *Memoir*, appears in Hallam Tennyson's printed but not published *Materials for a Biography of A. T.*, I, 246: "The termination [of 'The Two Voices'] as it now stands I first heard him read in my London chambers which I occupied for part of 1837 and 1838. Here too I heard him read the 'Talking Oak,' and the 'Daydream,' which had grown from three stanzas on 'The Sleeping Beauty,' . . . and I think also 'Locksley Hall.'" Since Lushington also records (p. 247) that he was not in London after early 1838, his recollection, if accurate, means that the poem must have been composed before that time; but we cannot be sure that it is accurate.

[54] *Memoir*, I, 150.

[55] One of the fragments of Tennyson's correspondence with Emily Sellwood printed in the *Memoir* under date 1838 reads: "I saw from the high road thro' Hagworthingham the tops of the elms on the lawn at Somersby beginning to kindle into green" (I, 167). Whether he stayed on the coast during this visit, we do not know, though he is not likely to have missed an opportunity to visit a seascape he loved so much (see *Works,* p. 916).

[56] Isaac Watson Dyer, *A Bibliography of Thomas Carlyle's Writings and Ana* (Portland, Maine, 1928), p. 8.

[57] In the extracts from Tennyson's letters to Emily for 1839 is the sentence: "Perhaps I am coming to the Lincolnshire coast, but I scarcely know." Three items down from this is an entry dated "Mablethorpe" (*Memoir*, I, 168).

[58] The engagement is reported in a letter from Tennyson's aunt, Fanny Tennyson d'Eyncourt, to her son George (December 26, 1837): "You have also I think heard of the Barings who live n^r. Spilsby: Two daughters are to marry Duncomb [sic] Shafto and Frances [sic] Massingberd the Clergyman of Ormsby" (L.A.O., T d'E. H/121/98). Since the d'Eyncourts lived some distance from Harrington, the rumor may have been current earlier in the Somersby neighborhood. But the Tennysons left Somersby some time in November, so that they may not have heard the news till later; Aunt Fanny wrote to George (November 29, 1837): "This curious family have left here & a happy deliverance" (L.A.O. T d'E. H/121/79).

[59] *Memoir*, I, 165.

[60] Lady Brougham's diary (see next note) shows that the engagement was finally settled in April.

[61] Lady Brougham, whose diary is now in University College Library, London, was Arthur Eden's sister. She saw Arthur a great deal during the 'thirties and after and sometimes records visits to and from other members of his family, but she seldom gives anything but a bare note of the visits (for example, "Arthur called and dined").

[62] Shafto was magistrate for Durham and Wiltshire, honorary colonel of the 2nd South Durham Volunteers, and from 1847 to 1868 a member of Parliament for Durham (*Times,* March 25, 1889, p. 9 f). Lady Brougham, in the passage in her diary quoted from above, says that she is "very sorry" Shafto had gone away because he is "so agreeable." We get another glimpse of his amiable character from a

letter written (probably in 1850) by Dulcibella Eden to Frank Charles Massingberd (L.A.O. Mass 4/98): "Ryde is very quiet now, but they have had plenty of sailing. M^r. Shafto says *he* would as soon be in Newgate and makes Rosa very angry, by asking, if the children and himself behave well the term of their imprisonment may not be shortened."

[63] *Six Tennyson Essays,* p. 102.

[64] Four lines of the poem ("Truth, for Truth," etc.) were written immediately after Lionel's death, and the whole poem was composed under the shadow of Tennyson's sorrow: "Sometimes when he was with us alone he would say, 'The thought of Lionel's death tears me to pieces, he was so full of promise and so young': and 'to keep himself up' he worked harder than ever at the new 'Locksley Hall' " (*Memoir,* II, 324 and 329).

[65] In the *Memoir* (I, 331) Hallam Tennyson applies the phrase "very woman of very woman" to Emily. It is also significant, I think, that the poem is dedicated to her.

[66] See James J. Hissey, *Over Fen and Wold* (London, 1898), pp. 340–341, and also William J. Monson, *Lincolnshire Church Notes,* Lincoln Record Society, XXXI (Hereford, 1936), p. 176. The resemblance between the Harrington monument and the one in "Locksley Hall Sixty Years After" has often been noted, particularly by the Rawnsleys (*Memories,* p. 5; *Tennyson and His Friends,* p. 25). There is a similar crusader's figure at Halton Holgate, the Rawnsleys' church, which Tennyson must also have known.

[67] Sir Charles (*Alfred Tennyson,* p. 211) says that the poem was written at Llanberis in 1845, but Hallam Tennyson quotes an 1839 letter from Tennyson to Emily Sellwood which reads: "The most beautiful thing I saw this time in Wales—Llanberis lakes. ('Edwin Morris' was written there.)" (*Memoir,* I, 174). The parenthesis is apparently Hallam Tennyson's and does not clearly say that the poem was written there *at that time,* but other evidence shows that it must have been. In the library of Trinity College, Cambridge, there are some manuscript fragments of the "butcher's book" which FitzGerald rescued before the publication of the 1842 volume and presented to the college (*Memoir,* I, 198; T.C. o.11a.5). These contain on one side what is labeled the "original draft" of "Audley Court" (written, according to the *Memoir,* I, 165, in the fall of 1838); on the reverse is a draft of "Edwin Morris" from the end of Edwin's speech. This evidence makes it almost certain that Hallam's record of the composition of the poem is correct.

[68] Harrington Hall is a large, handsome brick manor house dating from Tudor times but largely rebuilt in the late seventeenth century. The house in "Edwin Morris," however, is said to be "Tudor-chimnied," whereas Harrington's chimneys, I am told, cannot accurately be described as Tudor, though some informants of reasonable expertise have so characterized them. A full description of Harrington, together with an excellent photograph, is to be found in *Lincolnshire Notes and Queries,* VII (Horncastle, 1904), pp. 161–164.

[69] I have not been able to learn who Rosa's trustees were, but there is a good probability that her maternal uncle, Charles Edward Poulett Thomson (later Lord Sydenham) was one of them. Rashdall's diary records an 1834 visit of some length from the Poulett Thomsons to the Edens, and they may have visited in other years as well. The Poulett Thomsons were not cotton-spinners (for whom Tennyson seems to have had an extraordinary contempt; cf. *Maud*), but Charles Poulett Thomson was, all through the 'thirties, member for Manchester.

[70] See Edward Walford, *The County Families of the United Kingdom* (London, 1860).

[71] In the 1839 draft the conclusion of the poem ran:

But ere December came, my own suit fail'd,
Nipt by the true magician of the ring,
The rentroll Cupid of the rainy isles.
Tis true, we met: we kisst: swore faith: I breathed
In some new planet: a silent brother came
Upon us: ere a man could clasp his hands,
The cat was in the creampot. Out they came,
Trustees, & Aunts, & Uncles. "What! with him!"
"Go, Sir" & "collar him" and "get you in"
And "let him go." O facile nose of wax!
They wedded her to sixty thousand pounds,
To slight Sir Robert with his vapid smile
And educated whisker: but for me—
They set an ancient creditor to work.
I left the place, left Edwin; nor have seen
Him since, nor heard of her, nor cared to hear.
Yet comes at times a vision of the lake
When the prime swallow dips his wings or then
While the gold lily blows & overhead
The light cloud smoulders on the summer crag.

[72] A surviving manuscript of the poem (Harvard bMS Eng 952, No. 26, pp. 6–11), occurring with other poems of the early 1850's and different in detail from the published form, indicates that Tennyson was working on "Edwin Morris" right up to its publication in 1851. The manuscript breaks off with "Sir Robert and his watery smile," which suggests specifically that the published ending was not written till just before publication.

[73] See, for instance, E. D. H. Johnson, "The Lily and the Rose: Symbolic Meaning in Tennyson's *Maud*," *PMLA*, LXIV (1949), 1222–1227.

[74] In the Lincoln Public Library, tipped into a copy of George G. Napier's *Homes and Haunts of Alfred Tennyson*, is a letter from Napier to W. F. Rawnsley (dated Oct. 31, 1890), which reads in part: "In your last letter to me you said 'the high-hall garden is certainly Harrington.' I was greatly interested to hear this." But though Rawnsley's brother ten years after gave voice to the same opinion in his *Memories* (pp. 16–17), he himself went out of his way to deny the association in his lecture in 1909 at the Tennyson Centenary (*Ten-*

135

nyson, 1809–1909: a Lecture [Ambleside, 1909], p. 30), probably under pressure from Hallam Tennyson. Nevertheless, in his "Personal Recollections of Tennyson," *Nineteenth Century and After,* XCVII (Feb., 1925), 193, and in *Highways and Byways in Lincolnshire* (London, 1927), p. 340, he returned firmly to his old position. Both of the Rawnsleys described the carved paneled room in the Hall, but both are careful not to point out the similar feature of the Hall in *Maud* and neither makes any reference in discussing Harrington and *Maud* to the fact that Rosa lived there or to Rosa's association of herself with the "rose of the rosebud garden of girls." I for one find it difficult to believe that they did not see the obvious connections they overlook, especially in view of their other covert attempts to identify Maud with the Somersby-Harrington neighborhood (see *Memories,* pp. 19–20 and 46).

[75] The similarity between the garden of Harrington and the setting of "The Rosebud" and the garden passages of *Maud* is perhaps even more striking than I have made clear. Professor W. D. Paden writes me: "I do not think you make as much as you well might of the terrace at Harrington. . . . The terrace is, as I remember it, about eight feet high and ten feet broad, faced with brick along its sides, and extending for 75 feet along the western edge of the enclosed garden. When I saw it in 1959, the top was floored with slabs, between which roses bloomed, and there was a stone bench at the southern end, the end farthest from the house. A fine place for a young couple to walk in late afternoon or early dusk; conveniently private without any indecorous distance from the hall. To the west immediately under the terrace, a broad meadow with scattered oaks, a herd of black and white kine, and a view over the valley: 'The night with sudden odour reel'd, / The southern stars a music peal'd, / Warm beams across the meadow stole; / For Love flew over grove and field.' The *warm beams* I take to be candle-light from the hall's windows, radiating across the front lawn and out over the meadow. All this is peculiarly suited to the Harrington structure and situation."

[76] The present owners of Harrington, Commander Sir John Maitland, M.P., and Lady Maitland inform me that they had the tradition from the Rawnsleys.

[77] My informant is Mrs. G. Fenwick-Owen, daughter of Walter Hugh Rawnsley (Drummond Rawnsley's oldest son) and niece of H. D. and W. F. Rawnsley.

[78] Tennyson himself identified the birds as rooks (Anne Ritchie, *Records of Tennyson, Ruskin, and Browning* [New York, 1893], pp. 48–49). The Rawnsleys also make the association between the birds of the Hall in *Maud* and the well-known (in the neighborhood) rookery at Harrington. When I myself was staying at Tetford, about three miles from Harrington, I inquired of some inhabitants what the phrase "the Hall" would be taken to mean in the neighborhood and got the reply, "Why, Harrington." When I asked what directional preposition would be used in reference to Harrington, I was given Tennyson's phrase in *Maud,* "*up* at the Hall."

[79] The room, often remarked upon in books about the Lincolnshire

136

countryside, has its panels no longer, but the present owners have shown me photographs taken before they were removed, and assure me of the accuracy of W. F. Rawnsley's description of it as "an old oak-panelled room, mostly richly carved" (*Highways and Byways,* p. 340).

[80] Lady Brougham's diary shows that Eden was in London a good bit of the year, usually without his family.

[81] These memories became intertwined, I think, or perhaps had been associated from the first, with Tennyson's readings in Arabic romances and poetry, the influence of which on the poems studied here has been analyzed by Paden (see n. 13 above), pp. 92–94, and John Killham, *Tennyson and "The Princess"* (London, 1958), pp. 188–192, 195–197, and 211–214.

[82] Unpublished letter (June 8, 1854) now in the Duke University Library.

[83] Palgrave says that Tennyson recited the poem to him at Farringford in 1854 (see n. 29 above); and in the *Memoir* (II, 493) he says that "I spent some days at Farringford in September, 1854, when 'Maud' was in course of completion."

[84] The episode may be conveniently found in the Everyman Malory, I, 118 ff.

[85] W. J. Rolfe, ed., *The Poetic and Dramatic Works of Alfred Lord Tennyson,* Cambridge edition (Boston, 1898), p. 859 n. I should point out also that Tennyson gives Ettarre a garden ("all made up of the lily and the rose") which Malory had denied her.

[86] In "Aylmer's Field," which I have chosen not to examine at length, Tennyson builds upon Woolner's generalized reference to a cruel reproach which the hero suffered from the heroine's parents (*Thomas Woolner,* p. 220) a very vivid nighttime scene in which the hero, coming to meet his beloved, encounters instead her angry father and mother. Woolner's story, telling of the thwarted love of the boy at the Rectory for the girl at the Hall, must have struck a very responsive chord in Tennyson's heart.

[87] In *Maud,* "Edwin Morris," and "Locksley Hall" (if it was in fact written on the Lincolnshire coast) Tennyson used features of the landscape in front of him as he wrote. "Edwin Morris" reflects the scenery of the Llanberis lakes where it was written, and *Maud* draws heavily on the landscape around Farringford and Sir John Simeon's home at Swainston (*Memoir,* I, 402 and 513; V. Scott O'Connor, "Tennyson and His Friends at Freshwater," *The Century,* LV [Dec., 1897], pp. 249, 256–257). Building up his dramatic setting from such foundations, it was all the easier for him to bring in reminiscences, perhaps largely unconscious, of places and scenes the images of which had been fixed in his mind by long and powerfully stimulated association.

[88] Tennyson's troubled mood found expression also in a number of bitter jottings preserved in one of the workbooks of the 'sixties and printed by Professor Buckley in his study of Tennyson, pp. 163–164 (see n. 49, above). One, for example, runs:

I ran upon life unknowing without or Science or Art;

137

> I found the first pretty maiden but she was a harlot at
> heart.
> I wandered about the woodland after the melting of
> snow.
> There was the first pretty snowdrop—and it was the
> dung of a crow.

[89] Tennyson was always conscious of the ambiguities of romantic involvement and feared, like the hero of *Maud*, the "honey of poison flowers." He could not accept the animal basis of love; for him as for Lucretius "Twy-natured is no nature." And so in one of the *Unpublished Early Poems* (p. 55) he beseeches "Amy" to

> take blind Passion; give him eyes; and freeing
>   His spirit from his frame
> Make double-natured love lose half his being
>   In thy spiritual flame . . .

[90] The hero of "Locksley Hall" is "shamed thro' all my nature to have loved so slight a thing."

[91] In none of Rosa's diaries have I noticed any expression of religious feeling or spiritual or moral reflection, even in times of grief.

CHAPTER 3.

[1] Sophy was baptized October 27, 1818, according to A. R. Maddison, *Lincolnshire Pedigrees* (*Publications of the Harleian Society*, L–LII, LV), IV, 1302.

[2] See H. D. Rawnsley, *Memories of the Tennysons*, 2nd edition (Glasgow, 1912), p. 65. Tennyson said in his notes to "Lilian" and similar poems that "all these ladies were evolved, like the camel, from my own consciousness," which forced his son to add in a parenthesis that Isabel at least was more or less a portrait of the poet's mother (*Works*, ed. Hallam Lord Tennyson, single vol. edition [London, 1913], p. 895). Certain lines in a poem by Arthur Hallam (*The Writings of Arthur Hallam*, ed. T. H. Vail Motter [New York, 1943], p. 93) seem to imply that Madeline also was to some extent a portrait.

[3] From the original letter in the library of Trinity College, Cambridge, postmarked April 14, 1835.

[4] *Memories*, p. 68.

[5] *Ibid.*, p. 66; preserved in manuscript among the Tennyson papers at Harvard (bMS Eng 952.1, No. 239) as well as in the typed copy used by Rawnsley (see next note).

[6] *Ibid.*, p. 68 n. These are apparently typescripts preserved in the Rawnsley section of the Harvard Tennyson papers (bMS Eng 952.2, Nos. 29 and 32). Quotations are by permission of Harvard College Library.

[7] The letter is one of those described below now in the Tennyson collection at the Duke University Library.

[8] Sir Charles Tennyson, *Alfred Tennyson* (London, 1949), p. 233.

[9] Letter from Mr. Michael Reader, Sophy's grandson, to his cousin Robin Thoyts, Esq., who had solicited from Mr. Reader (on my

behalf) his knowledge of his grandmother's relationship with Tennyson; the letter, now in my possession, is dated November 9, 1959.

[10] Hallam Lord Tennyson, *Alfred Lord Tennyson: A Memoir* (London, 1897), I, 161. Hallam Tennyson does not say to whom the poem was written and in fact mentions Sophy only once in the course of the *Memoir*, when he prints Tennyson's letter of consolation to her on the death of her son in 1871 (II, 105).

[11] *Alfred Tennyson*, p. 233; see also the quotation from Mr. Reader's letter (above).

[12] Both letters are undated but appear to have been written in the spring of 1851.

[13] Both Emily herself and Agnes Weld imply that the families had known each other well before 1830, an implication which agrees with the fact (called to my attention by Professor W. D. Paden) that Emily's uncle and aunt, who were close to the Sellwoods, preceded the Edens in residence at Harrington Hall, neighboring Somersby. It is rather odd, therefore, that Alfred and Emily did not meet sooner. See *Tennyson and His Friends*, ed. Hallam Lord Tennyson (London, 1911), p. 4; Agnes Weld, *Glimpses of the Tennysons* (London, 1903), p. 2; and Maddison, *Lincolnshire Pedigrees*, I, 282.

[14] *Memoir*, I, 148.

[15] But the tenderness recorded in "The Bridesmaid" could scarcely have arisen without some previous intimacy, and Rashdall's reference to "the Sellwoods" (quoted above) seems to indicate that the family were familiar visitors at Somersby in 1834.

[16] *Memoir*, I, 150.

[17] *Alfred Tennyson*, p. 167.

[18] *Memoir*, I, 165–166.

[19] "Audley Court," "Walking to the Mail," "Edward Gray," "Godiva," "Edwin Morris" (in part), "Locksley Hall" (probably), and possibly other poems were written in this period.

[20] *Memoir*, I, 167–176; *Alfred Tennyson*, pp. 180–182. A few additional sentences are to be found in Hallam Tennyson's unpublished *Materials for a Life of A. T.* (4 vols.), I, 209–217.

[21] *Memoir*, I, 169.

[22] *Alfred Tennyson*, pp. 180–181.

[23] *Memoir*, I, 176.

[24] *Materials*, II, 38.

[25] *Alfred Tennyson*, p. 181.

[26] The last letter quoted in the *Memoir* (I, 175–176) refers to a visit with FitzGerald to Warwick Castle, which A. M. Terhune, *The Life of Edward FitzGerald* (New Haven, 1947), p. 120, dates in June, 1840. Tennyson's letter was presumably written not long after.

[27] Tennyson published "Love and Duty" in the 1842 volumes, rather more quickly than he was wont to publish personal poems, perhaps because he wanted Emily to see it there.

[28] *Memoir*, I, 176.

[29] *Alfred Tennyson*, pp. 179 and 240.

[30] *Ibid.*, p. 180.

[31] Lady Tennyson, in her brief "Recollections of My Early Life,"

sets down a few unpleasant memories of this maiden aunt, who was a prominent member of the Sellwood household during Emily's childhood but who lived apart from them after 1835 (*Tennyson and His Friends*, pp. 3–6). Tennyson's reference to the "crones" is made in a letter written in the fall of 1845 to T. H. Rawnsley; the phrase is omitted from the *Memoir* (I, 225–229) but supplied by Sir Charles (*Alfred Tennyson*, p. 207) from the MS letter, now among the Tennyson papers at Harvard (bMS Eng 952.2, No. 18).

[32] *Alfred Tennyson*, p. 181.

[33] Tennyson's sense of honor toward women was extremely punctilious: "'I would pluck my hand from a man even if he were my greatest hero, or dearest friend, if he wronged a woman or told her a lie'" (*Memoir*, I, 250).

[34] *Some New Letters of Edward FitzGerald*, ed. F. R. Barton (London, 1923), p. 19.

[35] *Memoir*, I, 166.

[36] Hallam Tennyson records that in 1842, for instance, Tennyson sent Emily, through his sister Emily Tennyson, a copy of a laudatory letter to him from Carlyle (*Memoir*, I, 214).

[37] *Alfred Tennyson*, pp. 186–188, and *Memoir*, I, 220–221.

[38] *Memoir*, I, 221.

[39] *Alfred Tennyson*, p. 198.

[40] *Ibid.*, p. 201.

[41] *Ibid.* A slightly different transcription of this letter is given by Terhune, p. 124 (see n. 26, above).

[42] *Alfred Tennyson*, pp. 127–128 and 199.

[43] *Memoir*, I, 17.

[44] *Alfred Tennyson*, p. 201.

[45] Wilfrid Ward, *Aubrey de Vere: a Memoir* (London, 1904), pp. 72 and 87. Of course Alfred's moods varied. A month earlier FitzGerald reported him in "good spirits" and working on a draft of *The Princess* (*Letters of Edward FitzGerald*, ed. W. Aldis Wright [London, 1907], I, 194).

[46] *New Letters and Memorials of Jane Welsh Carlyle*, ed. Alexander Carlyle (London, 1903), I, 180.

[47] *Alfred Tennyson*, p. 207.

[48] *Memoir*, I, 248 n.

[49] *Ibid.*, I, 249–250.

[50] *Alfred Tennyson*, p. 224.

[51] *Memories*, p. 72. "It has been one of my life's privileges," says Rawnsley, "to see the letters that passed in those days, before the marriage was arranged."

[52] W. F. Rawnsley, *Tennyson, 1809–1909: A Lecture* (Ambleside, 1909), p. 19. The date of the refusal is not clear in the printed *Lecture*, but I have seen a proof corrected by Rawnsley in which he adds the phrase "two years back," that is, from the time of Emily's letter —probably one of the "several letters written to my mother" about the time of the marriage (*Memories*, p. 125), possibly the April 1 letter, of which in the transcript the first part is missing (see n. 61).

[53] *More Letters of Edward FitzGerald*, ed. W. Aldis Wright (Lon-

don, 1902), p. 22; *New Letters*, ed. F. R. Barton, pp. 164–165.

[54] Ward, p. 146.

[55] *Materials*, II, 39.

[56] *Alfred Tennyson*, pp. 239–240.

[57] Unpublished letter, Tennyson to Catherine Rawnsley, Dec. 10, 1849 (Harvard bMS Eng 952.2, No. 7); the visit did not take place, apparently, till January (Tennyson to Catherine Rawnsley, Dec. 27, 1849; Harvard bMS Eng 952.2, No. 4) or perhaps even February (*Memories*, p. 122).

[58] *Lecture*, p. 23. Part of Emily's diffidence arose, no doubt, from her earlier refusal of Alfred, the circumstances of which she probably explained to Mrs. Rawnsley in the missing part of this letter (see nn. 52 and 61).

[59] *Alfred Tennyson*, p. 242.

[60] Emily was actually Catherine's cousin, but the two as children had lived together in the Sellwood household.

[61] *Ibid.* Hallam Tennyson says that the couple met at the Rawnsleys in the spring of 1850 (*Memoir*, I, 328), probably after this letter was received. The letter exists now only in a modern copy, with the first part of the original omitted (Harvard bMS Eng 952.2, No. 35); this and the other letters Emily wrote previous to the marriage (*Memories*, p. 125) were apparently destroyed.

[62] *Alfred Tennyson*, p. 243.

[63] *Lecture*, pp. 20–21. The letters from Mary Tennyson that Rawnsley quotes in this account are not among the Rawnsley portion of the Tennyson papers at Harvard; to whom they were addressed, how Rawnsley got them, and where they are now is a mystery.

[64] MS letter, June 14 [1850]; Harvard bMS Eng 952.2, No. 38. Quoted by permission of Harvard College Library. Rawnsley says that Emily refers here to (probably suppressed portions of) the April 1 letter (*Lecture*, p. 20).

[65] Unpublished letter now in the library of Trinity College, Cambridge, postmarked "Tx / My 7 / 1850."

[66] From "To the Vicar of Shiplake." Two versions of this poem have been printed, one by H. D. Rawnsley with the stanza quoted here together with another following (*Memories*, p. 75), and one by Hallam Tennyson without them and with other variants (*Memoir*, I, 330–331). The first was copied from Tennyson's autograph (now among the Rawnsley papers at Harvard, bMS Eng 952.2, No. 12), which, according to the account in *Memories*, the poet sent to Drummond Rawnsley six months after the wedding; the second version was, according to Hallam Tennyson, written and sent to the Rawnsleys by Tennyson immediately after the ceremony. But the letter from Tennyson to Catherine Rawnsley which Hallam quotes in support of his statement does not, in manuscript (June 14, 1850; Harvard bMS Eng 952.2, No. 38), contain the final sentence referring to the poem which Hallam gives, nor any other reference to it. Tennyson in fact could not have sent the poem after the wedding, for a line in the additional stanzas of the Rawnsley autograph copy clearly implies the six-month delay, and a covering letter by Tennyson (undated)

implies further that the Rawnsleys had not previously possessed any copy of the poem. Probably W. F. Rawnsley is correct in suggesting that Tennyson wrote the version given by Hallam just after the wedding but enlarged it six months later just before he sent the final version to the Rawnsleys ("Personal Recollections of Tennyson," *Nineteenth Century and After,* XCVII [Feb., 1925], 4).

[67] *Memoir,* I, 329.

[68] Quoted, as if from Alfred or Emily, in the *Memoir,* I, 332.

[69] Ward, p. 159.

[70] Basil Champneys, *Memoirs and Correspondence of Coventry Patmore* (London, 1900), I, 197.

[71] See *Alfred Tennyson,* pp. 259–276.

[72] Champneys, II, 304–305.

[73] Ward, pp. 227–228.

CHAPTER 4.

[1] The various manuscript drafts I have seen seem to show that Tennyson worked through the poem a number of times, writing new lyrics to fill in gaps, extending and revising the old ones. I have attempted no analysis of the process because the bulk of the MSS (at Trinity College, Cambridge) cannot be photostated or transcribed, a circumstance which makes it impossible to compare them with other MSS elsewhere.

[2] Where other references are not given, the reader may assume that this account of Tennyson's early life is based on Sir Charles' *Alfred Tennyson* (London, 1949).

[3] A series of curious incidents during Tennyson's father's trip to Italy in 1830 may have suggested the fall to death in *Maud* (see *Alfred Tennyson,* pp. 97–98); the "red-ribb'd" "hollow behind the little hill" has an analogue, as books on the Tennyson country have often noticed, in Holywell Glen, near Somersby, with its outcroppings of rust-colored rock.

[4] The phrase recalls Mrs. Tennyson's situation after the death of her husband. Tennyson wrote in 1833: "My mother, who as you know, is one of the most angelick natures on God's earth, always doing good as it were by a sort of intuition, continues in tolerable health, though occasionally subject to sick headaches and somewhat harassed with the cares incident to so large a family" (Hallam Tennyson, *Materials for a Life of A. T.* [4 vols.], I, 122, printed but not published). One source of her "cares" was the bonds exacted from her and her sons to cover her husband's debts (*Alfred Tennyson,* pp. 116, 157–158). These were the source of a great deal of resentment in the Tennyson family and were not finally discharged till just before *Maud* was written (unpublished letter, Frederick Rhodes to Frederick Tennyson, Oct. 25, 1853; Harvard MS Eng 933, No. 44).

[5] The applicability of the words to Tennyson is obvious to anyone familiar with his biography, but they are a particularly appropriate description of him in the middle 'thirties. Cf. his 1837 words to Milnes:

"a nervous, morbidly-irritable man, down in the world" and "stark-spoiled with the staggers of a mismanaged imagination."

[6] It was not, strictly speaking, a disinheritance, since Dr. Tennyson died before his brother and since the grandfather left to the Somersby Tennysons what he had intended for the father, the family estate as he had inherited it; Charles was left only the moneys and land which the grandfather had himself accumulated.

[7] Of Tennyson's extreme bitterness toward his uncle there can be no question. The brother's political prominence, his presence at "grand political dinners," his vanity and insolence, all tally with the figure the darkly handsome Charles d'Eyncourt cut in Lincolnshire. The sartorial excesses of Maud's brother (and her wealthy suitor) recall the extravagances of Bulwer-Lytton ("the padded man that wears the stays"), who was, of course, Tennyson's enemy and Charles' intimate friend.

[8] See *Alfred Tennyson*, pp. 16–21, 29.

[9] See *Burke's Peerage, sub* Boyne.

[10] William Russell, as appears from the d'Eyncourt papers, was a crude, hard-drinking man, not at all on good terms with his mother, of whom Tennyson was very fond. It is Russell who is referred to anonymously in the following passage of Allingham's diary: "T. said he had a rich cousin who drank hard and talked loud. 'He used to quote Byron to me—

        Over the waters of the dark blue sea—

and so forth, adding, "Poets have some sense." He offered to lend me Castle B[rancepeth] for our wedding month—"will you come down to B——? then you may go to Hell!" ' " (*William Allingham: A Diary*, ed. H. Allingham and D. Radford [London, 1907], p. 187). Hamilton (who did not succeed to the viscountcy until 1855) was greatly disliked by Elizabeth Russell, as the d'Eyncourt letters also show, and hence almost certainly by Tennyson. (When, in the 'sixties, Tennyson renewed acquaintance with the Boynes, after a long lapse, he remarked to Emily that "all went off pleasantly," as if he had expected that it might not—*Materials*, II, 399.) I rather imagine that some of the ill-feeling directed toward the suitor in both *Maud* and "Locksley Hall" relates as much to these two men as to Robert Shafto.

[11] Sir Timothy Eden, *Durham* (London, 1952), II, 345, 574. The building of Brancepeth occasioned an increasing intimacy between Charles Tennyson and Matthew Russell, which roused Dr. Tennyson's resentment and probably that of his family (*Alfred Tennyson*, p. 19). Tennyson was only nine or ten at the time, but "the persons and incidents of his childhood," according to Jowett, always remained "very vivid to him" (*Tennyson and His Friends*, ed. Hallam Lord Tennyson [London, 1911], p. 187).

[12] Hallam Lord Tennyson, *Alfred Lord Tennyson: A Memoir by His Son* (London, 1897), I, 407–408.

[13] On September 1, 1835, Charles Tennyson d'Eyncourt wrote to his son George: "I know no reason why any of that [Somersby] family shd be dissatisfied—my Father has done what he always said he wd

do, & this was well known to them all—& is the same as he would have done if my Bro[the]r had lived except that he has been *a Father* to the Younger Children. Alfred I find has been so violent (tho he gets the Manor [?] of Grasby & an Estate there) that Mr. & Mrs. Bourne sent him away from Margate where he was with them" (Lincolnshire Archives Office H/116a/34). A joint letter from Edwin Tennyson d'Eyncourt and Elizabeth Russell to Charles Tennyson d'Eyncourt was apparently prompted by an enlarged version of the same report; Edwin writes: "Your letter to my Aunt which she received last night has convinced me what *a hog* that Alfred is and what can you expect from a pig but a grunt. However I would not trouble myself by thinking about it. It is too contemptible a subject. As to his not seeing me, I can assure him that I feel excessively grateful for his decision on that point, because I would rather be excused meeting a bloated ploughman." But Elizabeth Russell writes: "Don't give credit to all you may be told respecting individuals of the Somersby family, I believe Alfred incapable of that which has been attributed to him—but these sort of representations are most harassing to your spirits, consequently to your health & I feel vexed *very much*" (L.A.O. T d'E. H/118/54).

[14] The grandfather's death, which fully implemented the long-standing *de facto* disinheritance of the Somersby family, served as the occasion of a reconciliation between the Russells and the d'Eyncourts, who had been estranged for some time before, so that Tennyson had all the more reason to think of them together in this context; toward the end of 1836, the year following the grandfather's death, the Arthur Edens, as Lady Brougham's diary shows, began to see Robert Shafto with some regularity.

[15] See Sir Charles Tennyson, *Six Tennyson Essays* (London, 1954), pp. 70 ff.

[16] *Memoir*, II, 35; *William Allingham: A Diary*, p. 110; James Knowles, "Aspects of Tennyson, II (A Personal Reminiscence)," *Nineteenth Century*, XXXIII (Jan., 1893), 169. The point was suggested to me by Professor Douglas Bush's discussion of *Lucretius* in *Mythology and the Romantic Tradition* (New York, 1957), p. 215.

[17] *Maud*, Tennyson told Van Dyke, "is the story of a man who has a morbid nature, with a touch of inherited insanity, . . . You must remember that it is not I myself speaking. It is this man with the strain of madness in his blood, and the memory of a great trouble and wrong that has put him out with the world" ("Voice of Tennyson," pp. 539–540).

[18] Mrs. Betty Miller (in "Camelot at Cambridge," *Twentieth Century*, CLXIII [Feb., 1958], 142–145) has commented at some length on Tennyson's relation to Hallam and has presented the friendship in such a way as to suggest that it was to some extent homosexually based. Admittedly a great many facts—the intensity of the attachment, Henry Hallam's apparently uncomfortable attitude toward it, some of the language in *In Memoriam*, and so on—support such an inference; and the following comment of Jowett's on Tennyson's attitude toward Shakespeare's sonnets would seem to hint delicately at

the same conclusion: "Once again, perhaps in his weaker moments, he had thought of Shakespeare as happier in having the power to draw himself for his fellow men, and used to think Shakespeare greater in his sonnets than in his plays. But he soon returned to the thought which is indeed the thought of all the world. He would have seemed to me to be reverting for a moment to the great sorrow of his own mind. It would not have been manly or natural to have lived in it always. But in that peculiar phase of mind he found the sonnets a deeper expression of the never to be forgotten love which he felt more than any of the many moods of many minds which appear among his dramas. The love of the sonnets which he so strikingly expressed was a sort of sympathy with Hellenism." (This passage, given in the *Materials*, IV, 460, is not printed in the *Memoir* or its companion volume.) On the other hand, we need to remember that such friendships as Tennyson and Hallam's were very common in contemporary Cambridge (see James Pope-Hennessy, *Monckton Milnes, The Years of Promise, 1809–1851*, London, 1949, p. 17), and that the language of *In Memoriam* was undoubtedly the effect of a tenderness released by the fact of death rather than an indication of Tennyson's attitude while Hallam was alive. "If anybody thinks I ever called him 'dearest' in his life," Tennyson said to Knowles, "they are much mistaken, for I never even called him 'dear'" ("Aspects of Tennyson," p. 187). I think it is safe to say that Tennyson's feeling for Hallam almost certainly had homosexual components, but that quite certainly he could have had no conscious awareness, or conception, of the possibility that his feeling could have been given physical expression; the very impossibility—the fact that the relationship was absolutely untinged by sensuality—was, as I suggest in the text, the very fact that made it possible for him to feel so deeply.

[19] The first phrase occurs in a passage quoted in the *Memoir* (I, 250) as illustrative of Tennyson's own deep convictions; the second occurs in the early poem "Amy" (*Unpublished Early Poems*, ed. Sir Charles Tennyson [London, 1931], p. 55).

[20] "A Farewell to the South," printed in *The Writings of Arthur Hallam*, ed. T. H. Vail Motter (New York, 1943), p. 20. The whole poem, and indeed a good deal of Hallam's writing, contains parallel and related sentiments.

[21] *Memoir*, I, 404.

[22] Henry Van Dyke, "The Voice of Tennyson," *Century Magazine*, XLV (Feb., 1893), pp. 540–541.

[23] *Memoir*, II, 466.

[24] Joyce Green, "Tennyson's Development During the 'Ten Years' Silence' (1832–1842)," *PMLA*, LXVI (Sept., 1951, 671), has noticed the similarity of some of the imagery in "O that 'twere possible" to *In Memoriam*, Section VII; another curious similarity is the idea of the phantom of the lost loved one as a "canker of the brain" in *In Memoriam*, Section XCII, and as "a blot upon the brain" in the lyric.

[25] *Tennyson and His Friends*, p. 232.

[26] *Memoir*, II, 319.

[27] *Memoir*, II, 477–478.

[28] *Tennyson and His Friends*, p. 233.

[29] The draft occurs in an early composition book in the library of Trinity College, Cambridge (0.15.32).

[30] Charles, as trustee, held the inheritances of the younger Tennyson children; they were extremely angry with him (as letters in the d'Eyncourt collection show) when, fearing for their interests, he delayed turning the money over to them for investment in Allen's scheme. Sellwood played the role of an intermediary in the negotiations, at one point offering to advance the money himself. Sophy's father, T. H. Rawnsley, was, as one of the children's guardians, also involved.

[31] See Sir Charles' "The Idylls of the King," *Twentieth Century*, CLXI (March, 1957), 281. Sir Charles is also correct, I believe, in thinking that the grandfather's refusal to subsidize Hallam's marriage to Emily Tennyson must be another ingredient in the poem; there, as in Tennyson's own case, the old man had been the economic opponent of love.

[32] Roy P. Basler, *Sex, Symbolism, and Psychology in Literature* (New Brunswick, N.J., 1948), p. 76.

[33] I think it significant that one of Tennyson's favorite verses (he wrote it out for Van Dyke after reading *Maud*) was this couplet from "Locksley Hall": "Love took up the harp of Life, and smote on all the chords with might; / Smote the chord of self, that, trembling, pass'd in music out of sight."

[34] This comparison is based on the assumption that "How thought you that this thing could captivate" (see p. 36 above) refers to Rosa; in the next paragraph the second comparison rests on a parallel assumption about "The form, the form alone is eloquent" (p. 131 n. 38).

[35] Looking over my remarks here and below on the pattern of the flower imagery in *Maud*, I perceive that I am indebted for important points to E. D. H. Johnson's "The Lily and the Rose: Symbolic Meaning in Tennyson's *Maud*," *PMLA*, LXIV (1949), 1222–1227. Cf. also Jerome H. Buckley, *Tennyson: The Growth of a Poet* (Cambridge, Mass., 1960), pp. 142–143.

[36] The three girls must have been closely associated in Tennyson's mind. He had known Sophy and probably Rosa from an early age; the two girls were very good friends, as were their fathers. Emily was related to the Cracrofts of Harrington; her family were friends of the Rawnsleys, and her cousin Catherine Franklin (who lived with the Sellwoods) married Sophy Rawnsley's brother. In the mid-'thirties Tennyson would have been seeing all three girls socially; in the space of one year (1836) he seems to have been to some extent drawn to all three.

[37] Cf. the closing lines of "Love and Duty."

[38] See Paull F. Baum, *Tennyson Sixty Years After* (Chapel Hill, 1948), p. 52, for a very perceptive comment; and Sir Charles' essay on "The Idylls of the King," p. 281.

[39] *Memoir*, I, 412.

[40] Cf. Baum, pp. 138–139: "The proper uses of morbidity and in-

cipient madness in poetry are difficult to determine, but few would look for them in the hero-soliloquist of a love tale. Such a hero, however, was a convenience to Tennyson when he chose to inveigh against mid-Victorian ills, for he could thus have it both ways: he could let himself go with all the elocutionary bitterness of "Locksley Hall" and he could pass off the outburst as dramatic, the raving of a 'morbid poetic soul.' "

[41] See *Aesthetic as Science of Expression and General Linguistic*, tr. Douglas Ainslie, 2nd edition (London, 1922), esp. pp. 21, 80–81; the earlier phrases in the sentence are adapted, as the reader will perceive, from Eliot, Wordsworth, and Joyce.

[42] See Basler, pp. 86–91.

[43] Tennyson's denials of the warmongering charges brought against him on the score of the poem by contemporary critics amount merely to this, that he and his hero favor war not as war but as a purgative moral crusade; he did not at all deny the sentiments voiced in the poem, nor did he wish to, because they were his own. A major instance is the reference to "This broad-brimm'd hawker of holy things, / Whose ear is stuft with his cotton, and rings / Even in dreams to the chink of his pence." The *Westminster Review* took this as a prima facie reference to John Bright, but Tennyson says in his notes, "I did not even know at the time that he was a Quaker" (*Works*, London, 1913, p. 958). Tennyson does not, one notices, deny that he nevertheless had Bright in mind, and even this equivocal statement is rather hard to reconcile with a later contemptuous reference in the poem to "the Quaker" who holds that war is sin. But there can be no doubt that the first reference is to Bright. Before the Crimean War and during it Bright was consistently in the public eye as the chief opponent of the war; his religious and humanitarian motives were, because of his position as a leading cotton manufacturer, often held to mask self-interested economic ones; his broad-brimmed hat was firmly established, by caricatures in *Punch* and other satirical references, as his trademark (see G. M. Trevelyan, *The Life of John Bright*, London [1925], pp. 107 n. and 225 ff.; Trevelyan assumes as a matter of course that the reference is to Bright). If there were any uncertainty about Tennyson's hostility to Bright, the following unpublished stanza from "The Penny-Wise" (printed in the *Morning Chronicle* three years before, when war with France seemed imminent) should remove it:

> Hush, babbling peace societies
>   Where Bright and Cobden trifles!
> Is this a time to preach of peace
>   When we should shriek for rifles?

(Harvard MS Eng 952, No. 26). Quoted by permission of Harvard College Library. The whole non-dramatic poem is quite in the same vein as the close of *Maud*.

[44] *Memoir*, I, 396.

[45] The interconnection of Tennyson's repressions and his nearly hysterical fear and hatred of foreign aggressors, especially those of darker races, is (it seems to me) aptly illustrated by Sir Charles' ac-

count of a conversation Tennyson once held with Gladstone: "The talk naturally turned to the case of Governor Eyre, whose conduct in suppressing the rebellion in Jamaica during October and November was being violently attacked and defended with equal violence by press and public. Gladstone was strongly against Eyre, and stated his case in an orator's tone, . . . Tennyson, who took the view that Eyre had been justified in the steps which he had taken to save European lives, did not argue, but kept on asserting prejudices and convictions: 'We are too tender to our savages—we are more tender to blacks than to ourselves . . . Niggers are tigers, niggers are tigers [in *obligato— sotto voce*].' Dr. Symonds interpolated that Englishmen, too, are strong and cruel, quoting instances. 'That's not like Oriental cruelty,' said Tennyson. 'I couldn't kill a cat—not the tom cat who scratches and miaows over his disgusting *amours* and keeps me awake!'—the last words thrown in with an indefinable impatience and rasping hatred" (*Alfred Tennyson*, p. 359).

[46] Quoted by Sir Harold Nicolson, *Tennyson: Aspects of His Life, Character, and Poetry* (London, 1949), p. 200.

[47] Some readers of my manuscript have thought this judgment of the *Idylls* unjustly harsh. Perhaps it is; but I leave it unchanged because, despite the testimony of critics like Sir Charles Tennyson and Professors Douglas Bush and Jerome H. Buckley, whose opinions I very much respect, it remains an honest reflection of my considered estimate of the poetic value of the *Idylls,* great historical monument though it is. A very helpful and balanced discussion of the value of the *Idylls* is offered by Professor Donald Smalley in "A New Look at Tennyson—And Especially the *Idylls*," *JEGP*, LXI (April, 1962), 349–357.

[48] *Tennyson and His Friends*, p. 186. The "circumstances" Jowett specifies as "the old calamity of the disinheritance of his father and his treatment by rogues in the days of his youth."

[49] Basil Champneys, *Memoirs and Correspondence of Coventry Patmore* (London, 1900), I, 198.

[50] James Knowles, "Aspects of Tennyson, II: A Personal Reminiscence," *Nineteenth Century*, XXXIII (Jan., 1893), 182; cf. *Memoir*, I, 305.

Index